Flea Market Jesus

Flea Market Jesus

Arthur E. Farnsley II

CASCADE *Books* · Eugene, Oregon

FLEA MARKET JESUS

Cascade Books
An Imprint of Wipf and Stock Publishers
199 W. 8th Ave., Suite 3
Eugene, OR 97401
www.wipfandstock.com

ISBN 13: 978-1-61097-985-6

Cataloging-in-Publication data:

Farnsley, Arthur E. II.

    Flea market Jesus / Arthur E. Farnsley II.

    viii + 120 p. ; cm. Includes bibliographical references.

    ISBN 13: 978-1-61097-985-6

    1. National characteristics, American Individualism. 2. United States—Social life and customs. 3. Christianity—21st Century. I. Title.

E169.12 F385 2012

Manufactured in the U.S.A.

Contents

Acknowledgments

THIS BOOK, MY FIFTH, is unlike anything I've ever attempted before. I hope it is smart, but it is not "scholarly." We all write what we know, but this book has enough autobiography to make me uncomfortable.

I am not uncomfortable, however, recognizing the people who support me in everything I do. This part is supposed to be personal. So thanks to my wife, Gail, and my daughters, Sarah and Caleigh, who are nothing short of everything to me.

Thanks also to my work family at the Center for the Study of Religion and American Culture (CSRAC). I undertook the research for this book before I joined the CSRAC team, but I've been among them while writing and rewriting it. So Philip Goff, Tom Davis, Peter Thuesen, Rachel Wheeler, Becky Vasko, and Joy Sherrill: thanks.

Thanks to all my friends at Friendship, both in the NMLRA and in the flea markets. Special shout out to Dan, Shane, and Mike, who make Friendship what it is. Thanks to my Old Mill friends Bill, Debbie, Michael Scott, Uncle Raymond, Jimmy, Toy, Peggy, Ginger, Kelly, and Paula. Thanks also to my NMLRA friends Melissa, Denise, Bones, John Gibbs, Navio, Larry, Todd, Chuck, Tim, Jeremiah, and Alliey. And thanks to everyone in the flea markets who took the time to talk to me. And to Harold, because Friendship needs a Bookman.

Two of my previous books were team efforts, and on one of those I was not the lead author. The other two books were monographs, but one started as a doctoral dissertation, so my committee was a built-in team of expert reviewers. My other monograph on faith-based welfare reform contained much information that appeared in academic journals and in various other publications, so much of it had been vetted thoroughly. What I'm saying is: "I've had a lot of help and oversight."

But this time, I am really on my own, which is a little unnerving but, as you'll see, is kind of the point. My friends at the Louisville Institute took a chance by funding me directly, as an individual who had no institution at the time, to undertake this project. I hope I've repaid their trust, especially the long-term trust of Jim Lewis. Jim will be followed as director of the Institute, but he will never be replaced.

I also need to thank the nice folks at *Christianity Today* for including my flea market article in their 50th anniversary issue. Thanks to Hartford Seminary for allowing me to teach an online class improbably named "Flea Market Jesus." And thanks to my friends at Wabash College for inviting me there to give the Eric Dean lecture, the first time I inserted myself into this story. Any book worth its salt has also had a good editor; many thanks to Rodney Clapp, my editor at Cascade Books.

Next to last, I want to thank Cochise. He was the first person I interviewed for this project. He has trusted me to put other people's words in his mouth here, and I sincerely hope he never regrets it. I want to be clear, as I hope I am in the text, that 60 different people said the words I assign to Cochise as a literary device. Moreover, some of the back story on the Cochise character in the book is close to his real life, but other parts are drawn from other people's stories. None of your business which is which, because, once again, the Cochise presented in the book is a composite, a character. But there is a real Cochise, he is the backdrop for what I've done here, I wanted to use his Friendship name for my composite character, he let me, and I thank him.

Finally, I need to thank my father, Dale E. Farnsley, and my stepfather, Robert J. Berger, whom I have always called "Pop." On the surface, they share the unique distinction of having married my mother. But they share many other traits too, including a rock-solid commitment to love and care for me as a child, a teenager, a young adult, and still today, plus a shared devotion to my children. A couple of Tuesdays each month now they meet for lunch; they call each other their "husband-in-law." Seriously. There's a lot of Dad in this book because, well, you will see why. But credit (or blame) for how I turned out goes to Pop, too. So thanks, guys. I will never forget.

1

Deeply Spiritual But Not Religious

A N EAGLE SPOKE TO my friend, Cochise. Well, a dead loved one spoke to him through an eagle. He was out on a lake fishing when the eagle swooped down and gave him the message that she was in a better place and doing fine and everything was okay.

Cochise's eagle story is not unique, or even very unusual. A lot of Americans—a lot—believe in the supernatural and interpret events in their lives as intervention by God or angels or deceased friends and relatives.

The majority of American believers are "religious," which is to say they subscribe, however loosely, to a recognized theology and are affiliated with a religious organization. They place their experiences of miracles or divine guidance in the context of other beliefs and practices in their religion. But a large minority of believers steers clear of organized religion or traditional theology, preferring to describe their experiences as "spiritual."

There is no stark line with the religious on one side and spiritual on the other. The space between religion and spirituality in America is a continuum and we can find people at every point along it. We know, or think we know, religion when we see it, but it is usually a mistake to assume too much. We may know someone is a Catholic, or a Southern Baptist, or a Wiccan, but this probably tells us much less about them than we assume.

Cochise describes himself as spiritual but not religious, and I'd say that's right. He doesn't belong to any church, synagogue, or mosque. He doesn't watch religious programming on television, visit religious websites, or read religious magazines. He thinks in terms of a Higher Power rather than God. But he experiences the world, at least sometimes, as moved by magical and supernatural forces.

What makes Cochise's spirituality and his experience of the supernatural different from organized religion and its supernatural elements is his incredibly high degree of *individualism*. Much American religion is individualistic, but Cochise has created his own mix of beliefs, emotions, ideas, experiences, and practices that are truly idiosyncratic: Cochise's spirituality is from, and about, himself. Religions make some claim to describe the world as it is for everyone, even if others fail to understand it that way. Religions employ shared myths, doctrines, ethics, symbols, rituals and so on to join the community in common beliefs and practices. Spirituality is highly individualistic. Little wonder it finds such a comfortable home in our highly individualized culture.

That America is full of individual spirituality is widely known. In academic circles, the most famous articulation of spiritual individualism comes in the form of "Sheila Larson" from Robert Bellah et al.'s *Habits of the Heart* (co-authored by my old graduate school professor, Steve Tipton). Ms. Larson described her own concoction as "Sheilaism," which has become the byword for all kinds of personally-constructed beliefs and experiences.

But Sheilaism became over-intellectualized through the years, not least because the intellectuals doing the reading and writing recognized this form of individualism in their own experiences and those of their friends. "Spiritual but not religious" became synonymous with people who felt some emotional attachment to transcendent truths but did not want to be associated with the doctrines, practices, or—God forbid—discipline of traditional religion and its leaders, theologies, and organizations. "Spiritual but not religious" became so trite it made its way into contemporary comedy. Daniel Tosh says when a young woman tells him, "I'm not religious, but I am deeply spiritual," he wants to reply, "I'm not honest, but I find you interesting."

American individualism, like American spirituality, is available in all sizes and colors, but I was drawn to the special brand practiced by Cochise and others like him for many reasons. I have spent most of my life studying religious organizations, the most visible, tangible form of traditional religion. I wrote a book about political changes in the Southern Baptist Convention, America's largest Protestant denomination. I wrote another about religious congregations as social service providers in federal welfare reform. A third was about the way religious ideas and organizations shape the culture of a city. All of these deal with religion in its traditional, most easily defined, form.

This time, I wanted to tell the story of people who were out there on their own, doing their best to live free from the constraints of religious organizations—or political or economic organizations, for that matter. I wanted the truest freelancers, the most rugged, independent individualists I could find. So this is a book about flea market dealers, people who work for themselves and do not participate much, if at all, in organized religion or government. Cochise is a flea market dealer.

I did not, of course, pick flea market dealers out of thin air. I could have picked artists or Harley riders or any number of other American subcultures that resist the normalizing, institutionalizing pressures of mainstream culture. And I did not pick flea market dealers because I adequately foresaw the coming Tea Party or Occupy Wall Street movements, both of which express some of the alienation I will be describing here.

I picked flea market dealers because I know them. Although the Cochise described here is a fictional, composite character, as I'll explain later, I've known the real Cochise for more than twenty-five years, all spent two weeks per year in the same flea market.

I know Cochise, and hundreds of other dealers, from Friendship, a village in Southern Indiana that hosts the twice-annual championship shoots of the National Muzzle Loading Rifle Association. Those shoots are surrounded by two flea markets that together have more than 700 dealers. But the shoots themselves are composed of other kinds of individualists, primarily people involved in the esoteric sport of black powder shooting, including those who still shoot flintlock rifles, and people involved in the even more esoteric hobby of buckskinning, specifically those who re-enact the period 1760–1840 on the American frontier. These other hyper-individualists are superficially similar to the dealers, but also different in important ways. Those differences make it difficult to stereotype this collection of white Midwesterners, no matter how tempting the prospect. If you think you've got them fully pictured as the "red state wingnuts" or "lumpen proletariat," I'm betting you are wrong.

Dealers

Flea market dealers provide excellent examples of individual, dislocated, spirituality because of their alienation from political and religious systems and their dogged determination to go it alone. They offer an extremely clear case of this alienation, but they are not unique. American culture runs along a spectrum with degrees of alienation common across the board. When we see tea partiers, libertarians, Wall Street occupiers, and populists we are seeing people who may not be out on the edge with the flea market dealers, but who share many of their anxieties and experience the same detachment.

Full-time flea market dealers live on the margins of America's political, religious, and economic systems. Most of us work in institutions such as corporations, small businesses, hospitals, schools, and, of course, government. Dealers work for themselves. Granted, the degree to which any of us is really integrated into our work environment varies and plenty of corporate or government employees feel alienated, but their lives are still embedded somewhere in the bureaucracy. Dealers have detached themselves, sometimes by their own choice, sometimes by the choices of others.

Most Americans think of themselves as part of a faith tradition and more than half are actually members of religious congregations. The dealers tend to go it alone on religion. Again, it would be unwise to overstate Americans' religious affiliation. About 95 percent say they believe in God or some higher power and something like 80 percent claim affiliation with some religion, but only about 55 percent belong to an actual congregation and more like 40 percent attend regularly, and an even smaller number—probably 25 percent to 30 percent—attend anything like "weekly." Still, flea market dealers are even less likely than average to be involved in organized religion or to be members of congregations. I pre-screened my interview subjects by asking how often they attended worship, not counting weddings or funerals. If they attended more than once or twice a year, I disqualified them. However, this rarely happened.

Most Americans lean toward the Republican or Democratic parties, or at least toward "liberal" or "conservative" points of view; the dealers fend off both party affiliations and ideological labels. They are not on anybody's side because, as they see it, nobody is really on their side. Most Americans know, however, that each year a slightly smaller number of people affiliate with the parties, choosing instead to call themselves independent.

On all of these scores, flea market dealers are the edge—I wouldn't say leading edge, but they are the least-engaged of a large group of people who are only loosely engaged in economic, religious, and political institutions. Are they angry? Some are. But I think a better word is *disillusioned*. A lot of dealers feel the system has screwed them somewhere down the line. They got fired, so they went to work for themselves. They couldn't take any more crap from their boss, so they quit and went to work for themselves. They got injured but their disability benefits aren't supporting them, so they went to work for themselves. You get the picture. It's a similar story for religion and politics: the system let them down or denied them full access in some way, so they turned their backs.

If you are not familiar with flea market dealers and don't know many of the present-day Tea Party supporters, you may think these folks are exactly one and the same. This is not true. Most Tea Party supporters want smaller government for tax reasons. Most flea market dealers pay no taxes. You do the math. The best predictor of Tea Party affiliation is a desire to have government be more Godly. Not true of dealers. I have certainly met dealers who are concerned about creeping socialism or Big Brother or President Obama being a secret Muslim or some such, but in general, dealers have a whole different set of issues. The alienation is related—they have this constant fear of an *inside* from which they have been left *outside*—but the demographics and the issues are not the same.

You might also assume that the dealers are really just a subset of the Red State Republicans, conservative and Christian. The dealers are different from the pro-capitalism, pro-defense, family-values Republicanism *precisely because they do not link their economic ideas to other religious and political ideas in a formal agenda.*

After World War II, southern populism became linked with Christian "premillennialism." Without telling a very long story, premillennialism is the view that the world will descend into chaos and the only thing that can save it is Christ's return, followed by his 1,000 year reign. When you see old books like *The Late, Great Planet Earth* or newer books like the *Left Behind* series, you are seeing premillennial theology at work. Postmillennialism, by contrast, sees the world moving in a generally positive direction for 1,000 years, after which Christ returns. These may sound like fairytales to some folks, but these stories play a huge role in the psyche of many Americans from poor to working class to middle class and even among some pretty educated, prosperous, folks. Anyone who does not understand how deeply embedded these myths are in the American psyche does not understand U.S. attitudes towards all kinds of things, especially foreign policy.

Populism separated from these religious ties has a certain optimism about life, and about the "good" kind of entrepreneurial capitalism, even if it views big business with a wary eye. But Southern populism linked up with premillennial theology to create a new kind of conservative Christian who was patriotic and pro-American—including capitalism—but concerned that the country was going to hell in a hand basket. What is important here is that a new, family-values Republican evolved in the south, changing the whole American political spectrum.

But not all Southern whites were swept up in that religious, family-values tide. Those who were further down the socio-economic scale were less likely to be involved in institutional religion: in short, they did not get the newsletters—any newsletters. The dealers are populists and they do have certain conservative religious beliefs, but these never aligned or coalesced for them, not least because they steered clear of the kinds of institutions and organizations that would crystallize their ideas and channel their energies. They are truly out there on their own.

I am drawn to the dealers, and always have been, because of their will to make a go of it on their own. I won't romanticize. The dealers are alienated from the institutions that shape our society and so, to some degree, are pushed to the margins by a system that routinely passes them by. A number of them are, I presume, cheating the welfare system or tax system, though I feel an obligation to say I don't really know this for a fact in any case—it's not the sort of thing anyone being recorded tells an interviewer, even an interviewer they have known for twenty years and are currently drinking a beer with. Whatever the case, they don't want to give in. They want to make a living, perhaps even create success, on their own terms—or as close to that as they can reasonably expect to come.

The dealers come from many different backgrounds. Few are college educated. Some are old hippies selling soap, potpourri, incense, crystals, Native American goods, or old books. Some are former laborers, often from long-gone manufacturing industries, who were introduced to a specific product line and found a cut-rate supplier so now they carry no-name tennis shoes, knock-off perfume, or diabetic socks.

Others have a limited skill, sometimes developed from a hobby. Perhaps they learned about antiques or pocket knives or learned to use a router to carve names and cute sayings into wooden plaques.

Their backgrounds are hardly monolithic so it's no surprise that their views vary too. Still, as I carried out my interviews and conversations, and later when I went back over the transcripts and the tapes, I discerned a story line I thought worthwhile. I decided to put the words to that story in the mouth of one speaker: my friend Cochise.

I've known the real "Cochise" for twenty-five years. He was also one of the first people I interviewed in my research because I knew he'd be interested in what I was doing, plus he could help by telling me if some of my questions did not make sense.

Cochise is not what it says on his driver's license, but is his Friendship flea market name, the one he goes by when he is dressed in his brain-tanned buckskin war shirt. The Cochise in this book is not really him, but a composite. I tried to distill a story line from my many interviews and then created a made-up character, based on my real-life friend, who would speak for the flea market dealers.

Every word of dialogue presented here was spoken by one of my flea market respondents. I did not invent a single phrase. Moreover, I am confident the dialogue accurately summarizes the thrust of the stories I heard. But it *is* a composite. The real Cochise said some of it, but so did dozens of other people, male and female, old and young. If this were a heavily sociological book, I would spend a lot of time analyzing the differences among my respondents. But in this case, I am arguing that these people represent a *type* of person and I am telling that story by combining emerging themes into one voice.

Like any writer, I am asking the reader to trust that I got the summary right. There can be no doubt that I have culled the responses, leaving out some minority opinions and highlighting quotations and ideas that make my point. But every author, no matter how disciplined in social-scientific approach, is making similar judgments and asking for the reader's trust. If I presented bits and pieces of dialogue from various respondents, you would never really know if I had chosen a representative sample of segments. If I presented every word verbatim from every respondent, you would never really know if I had chosen a representative set of respondents to interview in the first place. You have no choice but to see this story through my eyes.

I chose Cochise as the speaker because I wanted to make sure I was telling the story in the dealers' own words. Cochise is a mental check on my own analysis. For every analysis or opinion I add to what my subjects said, I can look in the mirror and ask myself, "Would it make sense to Cochise to hear me explain it that way?" Maybe when you hear a little about him you'll understand what I mean.

Cochise

You'd know he was once a heavy smoker even if you'd never seen him light up. His face has that blotchy mix of red and gray. His cheeks are hollowed, his eyes slightly yellowed and glassy. And his laugh is a deep, throaty wheeze. People all over Friendship know Cochise is near when they hear his pre-cancerous laugh.

I remember when he was a drunk. He'd tell you so himself. At Friendship he'd crack a beer as soon as he'd finished breakfast and would drink straight on through to evening. I never really counted how many he could drink in a day—who would?—but it was surely somewhere between 18 and a full case. In the morning, he'd offer a beer to close friends (most of whom—including me—would politely decline). By evening, he'd offer one to total strangers if they would sit and talk. I know he told himself that he only drank this much when he was on vacation, and many of the dealers view Friendship as a kind of break from their usual grind even if they work every day while they are there. But I also know that when he was finally arrested for being drunk and disorderly he was in a bar less than a mile from his house. He promised the judge he'd clean himself up, and he did.

Cochise is one of thousands of flea market dealers who took partial retirement based on disability at a relatively young age. These folks worked in a factory environment because they had to earn a living, but the moment they could get out—either through normal retirement or accelerated retirement through disability—they did. Among interview subjects who did not know me personally, the first question they'd often ask was, "are you from Social Security?" Apparently they'd always imagined someone might come along and ask them why they were able to do this flea market work, mostly without financial records, when they were receiving benefits because they could no longer do their old jobs. No one before me had ever asked them personal questions, so it stood to reason that I might be the person they'd been waiting for. In a very few instances I was turned away. My offer of $20 cash helped smooth some rough patches. And my beard and earring (and lack of black, rubber-soled, government agent shoes) probably persuaded a few that I was not an undercover welfare narc, if such a job even exists. I can tell you many dealers *think* that job exists.

Cochise worked many years for a large company with "General" in its name. He did skilled labor; he can assemble, weld, and do minor electrical repair. Because he was injured on the job, he was due a settlement. He wound up in court arguing about the amount and the conditions. But once he was out, he was not going back.

If you have any friends or relatives who do industrial labor for a living, then you know just how common this is. I have personally met dozens of the tens of thousands of people who have sued their employers. Not to blame the lawyers, but there is a reason all those personal injury law offices advertise during daytime television, and at 4:00 am. They are speaking to people who are not at work during the day and not getting up for work in the morning: a lot of those people think their former employers still owe them.

Eventually Cochise got his settlement. The details are not important here because no two stories are exactly the same and yet all of them are similar. He factored that in with his social security benefit to determine a baseline annual income, then decided to "go into business for himself" at the flea markets. He wanted to sell jewelry that he made from gold and silver. But not many flea market customers are prepared to pay what hand-made, precious-metal, jewelry costs, especially when the person hand-making them learned to value his time on a union scale. So Cochise began selling mass-produced knives as a way to create cash flow while he built up the jewelry business.

"Going into business for yourself" is a standard dream for working men all over America. Women may have similar dreams, but if they do, they say less about them (at least to me). Perhaps you saw the *Wonder Years* episode years ago where Kevin's dad takes the boys fishing and confides to them that he dreamed of buying the small bait store/grocery nearby and living out his days near the lake. His oldest son asks, "but don't you owe the bank a pile on the mortgage?" which broke the chummy mood. As men grow older, they learn to nod and offer mild encouragement when their buddies daydream out loud about things they will never really do. This is the same mental trick they play when buying guns they'll never shoot or knives they'll never use; the joy is in the escapism, in the mental image of what the person who owns this item is like. It's consumerism, but with dreams held in check by the reality of the situation.

For most people, the dream only becomes reality if they come into unexpected money through a disability payment, an inheritance, or the extraordinarily unlikely case of winning the lottery. And let's be honest, most working people don't stand to inherit much. Even in these rare cases of financial windfall, the results of "going into business for yourself" are often disastrous. The advice to "invest in yourself" is not always good, especially if "yourself" was not doing very well to begin with. Even lottery winners wind up owning money-losing gift stores selling useless crap because they invested in themselves.

A few dealers on disability make a fair profit, but most do not. The real profit-makers, the hustlers, are the ones who just could not stand working for a boss and who saw direct sales as a way out. Often they do not sell what they love because what they love is not profitable. They sell cheap Asian-made shoes or pieces of foam or off-brand tools. They are in business strictly to make money; their joy is not in their merchandise but in their independence.

Cochise tried to split the difference by selling mass-produced knives made by companies like Case or Buck. A few men buy these to use, but most buy them as ornaments, the way women buy ceramic figures or Longaberger baskets. One of the Friendship shoots is always the week before Father's Day, so kids often buy these affordable knives for their dads. Case makes its living selling commemorative knives that come in nice boxes with certificates of authenticity and serial numbers. These are "collectibles," something you own simply to own.

Is there enough mark-up in knives to ever make it worthwhile? I don't know and, at this point, Cochise may not really know either. He bought most of his inventory years ago. His display cases feature very few new knives, though he adds his own new jewelry from time to time, plus new knick-knacks he picked up on his travels to the desert southwest each winter. In the past couple of years I have bought a "desert rose"—a kind of gypsum crystal—and a gourd bowl lined with a design of beads secured with beeswax, both "finds" from his winter visits.

The problem with selling pre-made knives is that nothing distinguishes your merchandise from others in the market selling the same thing. You must either compete on price—which cuts your margins—or you try to make your merchandise eye-catching and then hope for the best. It is a not a high cash-flow business and the margins are not predictable. In short, it is not like soft-serve ice cream.

Cochise has a permanent residence, as most of the dealers do. Very few live only in the motor homes they drive from show to show. Many dealers have places, often mobile homes, out in the country. There are two reasons why so many people put mobile homes on rural lots. The obvious one is that the homes themselves are cheap; if the residents are not there year-round, why spend more? But the other reason is that property taxes are much lower if no fixed structures are built. Mobile homes, even with poured concrete porches, are not fixed structures.

Cochise lives downtown in the fairly large Midwestern city where he was born. He lives in a shotgun style house, one of many in a row built by the German immigrants of the late nineteenth and early twentieth centuries. Cochise owns the house now, but he didn't always. For years he was a tenant, then a handyman, then a friend and roommate, and finally a husband. Now he's a widower.

As a fairly young man, Cochise started living in a room he rented from an older woman who was recently widowed. He needed an inexpensive room, she needed the extra money for the mortgage. Through the years, they became friends. He would take care of things around the place—cut the grass and make repairs—in exchange for rent. In time, they became more like roommates. The mortgage was paid and he simply lived there with her, though she was older than his mother would have been if she were still alive. He used his own money to keep the place up with the understanding that one day he'd inherit it.

When his roommate landlord retired, she lost her health insurance. Or, more accurately, her annual contribution became too expensive. His ongoing insurance was guaranteed in his disability settlement. Although his policy would not cover a landlord or roommate or friend, it would cover a spouse. So they got married despite the fact she was more than forty years older.

Some might take offense at such a marriage of convenience, or at least find it odd, but no one should ever forget how forcefully people's choices are shaped by the demands of a bureaucratic and financial system over which they have no control. Facing an environment in which employers make the rules without having to defend how they fit people's lives, people re-shape their lives to fit the rules. And I can honestly say that almost none of the dealers I spoke with would condemn such a tactic. You've got to do what you've got to do. The marriage was legal, the bills got paid, and any cost was borne by the company, not by other working people, at least not directly. Case closed.

Sociologists have told us for several decades that the model of dad at work, mom at home, and the kids living with both parents was losing its descriptive power. In 2006, the "nuclear" family with mother and father both at home made up fewer than half of households in the U.S. for the first time. The flea market dealers still value the traditional, nuclear model, as they do most American ideals. They tell me about their grandmothers and grandfathers. But the dealers believe their "real life" to be very different. Most of the men have not held jobs that could independently support a wife and kids at home. Most of the women have worked in various roles all their lives. A large majority are divorced, possibly multiple times. Many have adult children, plus their grandchildren, living with them.

A lot of older flea market dealers have considerable responsibility for their grandchildren. I am always startled by how many of them financially support three generations. But for the most part, the kids stay with someone at a permanent residence somewhere. I have met only a few flea market dealers who keep small children with them, (mobile) home-schooling as they move from place to place. Many dealers are older, with indirect responsibility for their grown children. Many are childless or are non-custodial parents. It is hardly surprising that flea markets draw the kind of dealers who lack conventional, middle-class commitments to nuclear families, schools, churches, and work.

Cochise's marriage to his former landlord was his first; he never had children. He likes kids and always treated my children with care and concern. Recently, he started breeding and raising dogs—Chihuahuas no less. He carries them around with him in his motor home. His flea market neighbors are not always thrilled because even small dogs can be annoying when they start yipping. But when they were younger, my daughters would wander over to Cochise's for an hour just to hold and play with the dogs.

Like most of the dealers, Cochise is not college-educated. He graduated high school and worked construction. Eventually he was able to get a good union job at a factory. He lived a life much like the one lived by millions of other working Americans with one exception: he was truly on his own. Cochise lacked the tight relationship to his parents and to siblings—except for one brother who died young—that characterizes so much middle class life. He developed no close ties to churches, civic groups, or other organizations outside his company. Even his relationship with his employer ended in a messy divorce. His truest friend was his landlord, who eventually became his spouse. Many of the flea market dealers have this same experience of separation and isolation. They live outside the walls of the institutions and relationships that form the boundaries for most of our lives.

My flea market friends are who they are and I take what they say they believe at face value. I have no interest in trying to say whether they *really* believe these things or to psychoanalyze *why* they do. I have done my best to take them at their word and to reproduce those words faithfully.

At times I'll try to map out the rich traditions from which the ideas presented here stem, but identifying those roots does not explain away anyone's ideas or opinions. I am even less interested in reducing my friends to products of their social class or education. They were subjects in this project, but they are not objects. I have no doubt that each of us holds ideas and opinions shaped by our relative position in society, but this is no truer for Cochise, or for any of my respondents, than for the pope, the president, or me. Each of us is socially constructed by many different forces of economics, politics, culture, and ideas. None of us wants to be put in an analytical box and, let's be honest, none of us fits in those boxes as well as politicians, sales people, and academics wish we did.

Rather than trying to explain Cochise, I simply want to try to place him on the American cultural map. If we drop the intellectual presumption that we know all about him because of his social situation, if we lose the pretension that we can predict how he votes by knowing where he stands on "God, Guns, and Gays," then perhaps we can hear him speak for himself in ways that tell us something about ourselves, about where *we* are on that same map. At the very least, I know I learned something about where I am.

This is not esoteric research about an exotic subculture. Millions of Americans live largely outside the normal, middle-American institutions of business, government, religion, and nuclear family. Many mainstream assumptions about their religious and political beliefs are wrong; this is a small contribution toward setting the record straight. But beyond that, I hope that hearing the *dealers'* assumptions about American middle-class life will cause others to ask hard questions.

Neither is this a romantic rehearsal like *Forrest Gump*. There is no presumption here that the poor and poorly educated nurture some secret, naïve truth that we all knew in kindergarten but have subsequently forgotten. But there is a presumption, one I try to live my life by, that everyone's story counts the same. I realize the story of Cochise will not cause everyone to see themselves in it to the same degree it does for me, but I think it needs to be heard both for what it says about the flea market dealers and for what it says about the American experience.

Through My Eyes

Why do I feel I have to tell this story at all? There are many reasons, so impossibly intertwined that I will not even attempt to pick them apart. First, I think the media and the academic world have done a poor job of helping us all understand the range of religious individualism in America. Many surveys now show that the percentage of people who say they have no religious affiliation has moved close to 20 percent. It is headed higher.

But we are too often left with the misleading impression that these folks have no spiritual focus at all. I'm convinced the majority of them do. Moreover, I think most of them are Christian and would define themselves as such if pushed toward it; they just do not affiliate with any Christian group.

Second, when we hear "deeply spiritual but not religious" we tend to think of mysticism, non-Western religion, yoga, and a host of other practices falling outside the traditional religion we think of as normal. But I think a lot of that non-religious spirituality conceives of itself as Christian—even conservative, even fundamentalist, Christian—it just does not want to be institutionally defined. So I wanted to learn about people whom I knew did not involve themselves in any religious or spiritual institutions—or any institutions at all if they could help it.

Third, I wanted to know about the linkage between political, economic, and religious individualism. There's a lot of libertarian, market-oriented politics out there, but also a lot of populism, a great deal of covert Moral Majoritarianism (what one wag called Tea-vangelicalism) alongside a lot of religious individualism. I tried to find the most individualistic people I could to try to see how these different ideas linked up.

Fourth, I have been observing and talking to flea market dealers for decades, so this was the chance of a lifetime. Writers are told to "write what you know," and I know about this. I've written other books, but those were academic arguments framed within a specific literature. Here, I wanted to study, and to write, more from the ground up.

The fifth point is where it gets tricky, and I can't explain this one in a couple of sentences. I felt called to write about the dealers, drawn to tell this story. And to understand that, it would be useful to know a little more about me.

I come from the same stock as most of the dealers I interviewed. My people are from southern Indiana and central Kentucky. I was raised in a very traditionally religious environment by folks who were politically conservative on nearly every score. I grew up with both God and guns, and both figure prominently in the story I'm telling here.

But my life took a different turn. At an early age my parents and teachers realized I was bright and I was "tracked" onto the intellectual high road. Every advanced or accelerated class was for me. Everyone assumed I'd go to college and then to professional training of some sort. And I did. I went to Wabash College in Indiana, then Yale Divinity School, then Emory University for graduate school. I became a researcher in the field of religion and society. I wrote books about the internal politics of the Southern Baptist Convention, about government's attempts to use congregations for faith-based welfare reform, and about the ways congregations function in communities undergoing large-scale social change. I even co-authored a book about the religious make-up of an entire Midwestern city.

I have never denied that I studied religion as a means of working out my own religious ideas and feelings. Like many people—heck, most people—I got my earliest religious training from my mother. So a huge portion of my life has been trying to understand religion—in the world and in myself—through research, writing, and teaching.

But life takes funny turns and most of us experience continuities even as we change over time. For me, part of the continuity was attending the annual shoots of the National Muzzle Loading Rifle Association with my dad. When Dad was laid off from the public service utility, he even became a flea market dealer for a while, which is how I met many of my interview subjects twenty years or more before our formal interviews. My dad never went to college and most of my work seems esoteric to him. But at the shoots, we literally get to play out a parallel story, living a story that might have been the dominant narrative in our lives but in fact became a sidebar. And let me be honest: a lot of this secondary narrative revolves around guns.

So perhaps now you see where this is headed: a life's vocation chosen because of the religious and political passion passed down to me by my mother; an avocation—and even a vacation—revolving around the more masculine interests of my father; and an interest in politics bequeathed me by a grandfather and a mother who both held local elected office. I am a political individualist, a religious seeker, and a shooter, but not in equal portions. This is the story I have to tell.

As I say, perhaps now you can see where this is headed, which puts you years ahead of me. I spent a long time working on this project before I realized just how much it was about me, my own political views, my own spirituality, and even my relationship with my dad. I still think it's a good story, it just turned out to be my own story a little more than I originally envisioned.

2

Friendship

FRIENDSHIP IS THE SETTING for much of this story, which is less abstract than it sounds.

Friendship is a village in southeastern Indiana. Just outside the village sits the headquarters of the National Muzzle Loading Rifle Association (NMLRA). Twice a year, for nine days at a time, the area hosts the NMLRA's national shoots.

It is hard to know how much to tell you about Friendship. I need to tell you enough that you will know Cochise, the dealers in general, and me. I want to tell you decades of stories and remembrances in painful detail.

I was only twelve the first time I walked Friendship's gravel corridors in 1973. I proudly, unselfconsciously, carried a small, single-shot, .22 caliber rifle called a Stevens Favorite. Dad shouldered a 100-year-old, double-barreled, muzzle-loading shotgun that sits today in a safe in my house. Grandpa held a .39 caliber squirrel rifle that was converted from flintlock to percussion well before the Civil War, a gun nearly too heavy for me to lift at the age of 12. We were showing off because we had the good stuff.

We had been told, correctly, that many visitors carried antique firearms as they walked through Friendship. We thought our guns would be conversation starters—which they were. But frustrated looks from inquiring dealers taught us this was not show-and-tell. In Friendship, as in gun shows or flea markets across America, a gun making its way up and down the aisles is generally for sale. Otherwise, you're wasting everyone's time.

It was 1984 and I was twenty-three years old, a divinity school student at Yale University, before I visited Friendship again. Dad got laid off at the power company and was selling regularly in flea markets around Indiana. He and grandpa had been "setting up" twice a year at Friendship, nine days at a time. Dad bugged me to come spend a week with them. In 1984, I spent my first full week in one of the flea markets surrounding the "shoot."

Everyone simply says "Friendship" because that is the name of the town where about 60 people live. Friendship is on Indiana Highway 62, between Dillsboro and Cross Plains, nearest to Farmers Retreat. Google maps makes places like Friendship much easier to find nowadays.

It's a modest town: a bank, a tavern, a garage that still works on cars in addition to selling gas, and a general store that rents videos, heats frozen pizzas, makes excellent cold sandwiches, and sells hand-dipped ice cream impossibly cheaply. A few antique shops have come and gone through the years. These may not sound like much, but without the NMLRA and its twice-annual shoots, Friendship wouldn't even have these. As in so many Hoosier towns, the houses are well-kept but the public buildings look tired and worn.

Loughery Creek winds its way along Highway 62, though I suppose it would be better to say that Highway 62 was built along Loughery Creek. (I've heard every pronunciation for the creek, but the leading candidate sounds like "Laurie.") The creek can be very picturesque—rocks, eddies, slate and shale. It can also be a nightmare. Twice since I've been going to Friendship the creek has flooded catastrophically—once during the shoot itself. Erosion cuts gullies six feet deep. Large, metal campers are washed away. The questionable sanitation situation goes from risky to dangerous.

There is just one church in Friendship, curiously named Bear Creek Baptist—curious because there is no Bear Creek nearby. You can't park in their lot on Sunday mornings, but other times you can park there for a free-will donation.

That's the town. But when I say Friendship, or when someone says to me, "see you at Friendship," we're really talking about the national shoots sponsored by the NMLRA, whose offices are just east of the town. The NMLRA has about 17,000 members who collectively own 500 hundred acres containing several different shooting ranges and campgrounds.

For one week in June and another in September, the national shoots transform this quiet Hoosier corner into a black powder Woodstock.

The NMLRA is dedicated to "the understanding of, ability in, and marksmanship with early American muzzle loading firearms." So during the week-long events twice a year, a couple of thousand members gather to shoot, to discuss gun craftsmanship, and to sell guns or other equipment related to muzzle loading firearms. This interest in American history extends not only to antique weapons and accoutrements, but also to modern replicas and the entire range of historical re-enactment. Up on the hillside, across Highway 62 from the main shooting lines, sit the tipis and lodges in the enclosed campground and shooting range known as "Primitive." Folks there wear buckskin trousers and gingham dresses; during the shoot they live—to greater and lesser degrees—as pioneers would have lived prior to 1840. Many practice real-life frontier trades such as blacksmith, weaver, and horner (makes powder horns). Some make their living primarily selling goods to other buckskinners. It's not that they avoid the trade of tourists, but few outside this subculture would pay thousands of dollars for a rifle or hundreds for a well-made, engraved, powder horn.

The NMLRA owns several campgrounds. There is a full-service campground with all the hook-ups, to use the recreational vehicle lingo. There are several campgrounds where members can hook their trailers to electricity only. Their water and sewage must be self-contained, or they can use the plumbed bathhouses on the grounds. And then there is the primitive campground where everything from tents or tipis to cooking gear, bedclothes, and lighting is supposed to be a replica of pre-1840 items. Although I spend most of my time up in the primitive area, I own a small trailer, a 1975 white-and-turquoise Scotty, that stays on the ground year-round. It's only 10 feet long and 8 feet wide inside, but it has a small refrigerator, window air conditioner, and room to sleep three if they don't value their privacy. It works for my daughters and me. My dad (who snores) has his own trailer in the adjoining camping space and a big tarp between us creates our living room.

The Friendship shoots would be a spectacle if only NMLRA members and their families attended. There are separate events for every kind of muzzle loading rifle, shotgun, and pistol. There is trap, skeet, and more than one kind of woods walk, where contestants shoot at mannequin targets sited among the trees. There are side events for knife and tomahawk throwing, and for primitive bow. In the Mountain Man match, competitors must wear pre-1840 clothing while throwing knife and hawk, starting a fire with flint and steel, and shooting so accurately that the best can split a ball the size of your fingertip off of an axe blade in order to break clay pigeons placed on both sides. (I've seen this done many times, but it would be a damned lucky shot for me.)

Because the shoots create such a spectacle, however, the members need not worry about being alone. Hundreds—on weekends, thousands—of tourists drive the only state road in or out of town to watch. Two large flea markets have grown up on either side of NMLRA property and each operates its own campground where visitors who are not NMLRA members can stay. Hundreds of flea market dealers set up tents or campers directly on their sales sites; the bigger market has about 500 dealers and is one of the largest in Indiana. Food vendors, the same ones you see at the carnival, come along to sell elephant ears, barbeque, and ice cream. On weekends, Harley-Davidsons line the town's main street as bikers ride in, have a couple of Buds—occasionally more than a couple—on the tavern porch, and then ride back out.

This is the Friendship I remembered from that childhood day-trip with dad and grandpa in 1973: tipis, bearded mountain men, bikers in leathers, and the literally constant sound of gunfire because the earliest rifle matches begin at 8:00 am and the final shotgun matches, often conducted under the lights, don't end until 10:00 pm. This is the Friendship I returned to in 1984, by then an event my dad had become part of. And it is, to be honest, the Friendship I re-enter every June and September to this day. People will tell you it has changed—and doubtless it has—but when my nineteen-year-old daughter camps with me and her grandpa, she is surrounded by tipis, bearded mountain men, bikers, and the gunfire that still hurts her ears if she gets too close to the line.

When we first visited back in 1973, *we* were tourists who didn't know better than to carry firearms that were not for sale. To a twelve-year-old boy seeing it for the first time, Friendship is exciting and frightening. I saw it through a prism, the way I see a foreign country today while on vacation. But to my nineteen-year-old daughter, Friendship is part of the annual cycle sure as Christmas, Thanksgiving, and New Year. When she is there she wears pre-1840-style cotton print dresses, throws tomahawk, and even shoots black powder on occasion. She knows what is for sale and where. Both she and my older daughter are regulars, carrying on a tradition that began when I finally joined my father and grandfather. Even after my dad got back on with the utility company, we would return twice a year to Friendship. During the two years my family lived in England I only made it back for one shoot. Otherwise, not a year has passed that I have not attended at least one, and usually both. After all those years of my dad hoping guns would forge a bond between us, as they had between him and my grandfather, here was a place where they did—for precisely two weeks out of the year so long as neither of us asked ourselves too many questions.

Because I had started coming to Friendship once a year for eight years while we lived in Atlanta, I was a Friendship flea market regular by the time I moved back to Indiana in 1994. But I was still an outsider within the shoot itself even though I was an NMLRA member. I had been camping with my dad and grandpa in a camper inside one of the flea markets; I wasn't staying on NMLRA property or participating in the events. Plus I was getting bored. The flea markets change less than you might expect from year to year and Dad and I had pretty much exhausted our ability to find enough conversation topics to cover a week of camping.

But this bond with my dad was so efficient, and so much more fun than other things we might be doing together, that I hated to give it up. It involved lots of beer drinking and gave me a chance to hang out with people much different from my university colleagues. (And believe me, we do not refer to one another as "colleagues" in Friendship.) It offered quality time with dad that had clear boundaries: we both knew when Friendship started and ended. My wife, who doesn't care for guns or rednecks, could remain completely uninvolved without any hard feelings. After all, dad's second wife never came to Friendship either. It was a nearly perfect father-son situation, a weeklong vacation from the rest of our lives where I could also be, to at least some degree, the son my father always wanted. But I needed some way to make the whole week more interesting for me. Ultimately, I did what any good son would do: I took up tomahawk throwing.

Without trying to sound more-homespun-than-thou, I confidently claim to be one of the few Yale Divinity School alumni or Emory University PhDs who dresses in buckskins and throws both knives and tomahawks at slabs of wood. I took up tomahawk for practical reasons:

the level of competition is much less stiff than it is for shooting sports, the buy-in cost is low, and I can practice in my backyard.

I'm hardly the first person to have the idea. Every year dozens of Friendship tourists see the throwing events and buy themselves a hawk. But unlike me, they don't have a longstanding commitment to return for both shoots every year with their dad. Most probably throw the hawk a time or two, put it on a shelf somewhere, and forget it. Not me. I threw a lot.

I started out with a hawk made by my dad, pounded and welded from a piece of metal pipe with a broomstick segment as a handle. Fortunately, the guy who set up next to us in the flea market—Dave—saw that this arrangement was not really going to work. At best, I wasn't going to be a very accurate thrower. At worst, I was going to humiliate myself as the Yale guy who threw a dull-edged tomahawk with a broom-stick handle.

Dave was something of a buckskinner himself even though he camped at his flea market booth and not in Primitive, mostly because it was much cheaper to camp in the markets, because if you camp on the land where your booth sits, the camping is free. He took me to the hawk range and showed me how far we had to stand—at least 12 feet—and how best to hold and release the hawk. Then he took me across the road to buy a top-quality weapon from H & B Forge. I think I paid $30. Even today you can get a top of the line hawk from H & B, or Beaver Bill's Forge, for about $50. These are the absolute real deal, pounded out by a blacksmith, with a blackened finish, smooth edge, and *almost* unbreak-able hickory handles.

By 1995 I was going to the knife and tomahawk range regularly during the shoots but, more than that, I was throwing for a few min-utes at home four or five nights a week during the spring, summer, and fall. It was therapeutic. After I had a tense day at work, I'd come home, crack a beer, and throw hawk for fifteen minutes. Because some of the hawk events had to be thrown while wearing "primitive," pre-1840-style clothes, I gradually developed a wardrobe. I bought a kind of starter set, including a pair of cloth knee breeches with bone buttons and a white, blousy, linen shirt. Dad bought me a pair of elk-and-deerskin moccasins sewn by the legendary Paul Poppen of Gatlinburg, Tennessee.

In 1995 I won my first medal, a bronze, in a tomahawk event. It was a fluke—I had good luck in an event that could not be re-entered. You throw at ten targets ranging in size from the bottom of a Coke can to the diameter of a quarter. No do-overs: it is all or nothing the first time through. I think I hit three, but three was good enough for the bronze because this is really difficult.

I took up knife throwing because knife events take place simultaneously and there is a combined competition. My first knife was forged from the rear main spring of a car by Steve Baxter, a Tennessee blacksmith, crack shot, and expert knife thrower. In a world of make-believe mountain men, Steve is as close to the real deal as you are likely to come in this day and age, complete with long, gray beard, buckskin leggings, and steely blue eyes. The knife he made me had a wrapped rawhide handle. My daughters throw it today. Even my girls will tell you, there is little in life more satisfying that the "thttt" sound the knife make when it sticks solid. Although I've decided not to use Freudian analysis on my dad's gun attachment, I'm not tone deaf to what my knife-sticking satisfaction says about me.

At around the age of seven each of my daughters began throwing tomahawk with me. This is a minor hobby for them, as for me—something to do while we camp with their grandpa at Friendship. They both got pretty good and often won the junior girls competition and went on to win a few women's competitions too. As I write this, I have won more than 100 medals and 22 combined knife and tomahawk championships; I hold the NMLRA national record as the only person ever to throw a perfect score on the tomahawk targets that have been used since the 1970s.

To picture those targets, think of a three of Spades. The target card is slightly larger than a playing card, and instead of spades there are three nickel-sized dots running down the middle, four inches from top to bottom. The goal is to stand at least twelve feet from the target and put the blade on all three dots. There are five throws in a match. I'm the only person ever to hit all three dots in all five throws. As Yogi said, "you can look it up." If you ever come to Friendship—heck, if you ever get on the NMLRA website—you'll see my name in the "Record Scores" section of the shoot program.

My daughters and I are Friendship regulars now by any measure. They started camping with me around the time each turned six. They stay with me in the Scotty camper parked just outside the Primitive gates. We wear primitive clothing most of the time we are there—I long since graduated to buckskin britches of my own—and we regularly take part in the competitions. In fact, my youngest daughter is the record holder in junior girls knife throwing. I now shoot flintlock rifle and primitive bow too, but with considerably less success than I've had in knife and hawk. We have groups of friends in the campgrounds, up in Primitive, and in the flea markets, all of whom we look forward to seeing every year. My daughters and I knowingly refer to the thousands of day-trippers as "tourists."

I've been going to Friendship more than twenty years now, and I'm analytical by nature and by profession, so of course I've analyzed the social setting using my own social-scientific lens. For many of the Friendship regulars, life at the shoot is not so much different than life the rest of the year. Some of the buckskinners travel around the country attending "rendezvous" where they sell primitive camp gear, knives, guns, blankets, beadwork, or any of the hundreds of supplies—all but the gun are usually referred to as "accoutrements"—that make up the buckskinning or rendezvous subculture. Others are gunsmiths who take orders for custom-built rifles and make their livelihood at that craft. A top of the line flintlock rifle can cost several thousand dollars; I paid Mike Brooks of Davenport, Iowa, $1900 for mine in 1999. It has the highest quality curly maple stock and the best metal work, including locks and barrels, right down to my initials monogrammed on the thumb plate. It is a *much* better rifle than I am a shot.

For the gun builders and accoutrement makers, Friendship is work. They come to buy, sell, and take orders. But even for those who do not work directly in the black powder trade, Friendship is like a giant version of the shoots they take part in regularly at their local clubs. Others attend primitive rendezvous throughout the year, so Friendship is the carnival version. Many of the participants arrange their free time around shooting just as golfers do around their game.

For most of the flea-market dealers who set up on the outskirts of the actual shoot, this is just one stop—albeit a favorite one—on an endless circuit. Some of the dealers come to Friendship primarily for the festival atmosphere and because they have had the same friends there for decades. Long after he went back to his full-time job, Dad planned his vacation so he could set up at Friendship. But for most dealers, these two weeks are on the job. Fortunately for them, Friendship provides some diversions, including nightly live music at both markets, which other markets don't always have.

Three Subcultures

Three different subcultures come together in the Friendship experience: shooters, re-enactors, and flea market dealers. Beyond that are the tourists and day-trippers, including the bikers. The bikers alone would be worth studying, but bikers ride to lots of sites, so nothing makes Friendship unique in Harley culture.

I camp now with the shooters, and compete with the primitive re-enactors, the buckskinners, but my fascination is with the flea market dealers. For years I camped in one of the flea markets, often as a dealer with my dad. I stopped camping there for practical reasons: I can leave my trailer on the NMLRA grounds year-round—no towing—and it's a very short walk to the tomahawk range where I spend lots of time during the day.

Of the three groups, the shooters are the most mainstream. A lot of them are skilled tradespeople—carpenters, draftsmen, plumbers, contractors—and virtually all of them are fiercely independent. Ask yourself: who wants to go to the trouble of shooting a muzzle loading firearm that is inherently less accurate and much more difficult to load and clean than contemporary guns? The answer: people who like working with their hands and enjoy the technical challenges of something so esoteric.

You are probably picturing the shooters already, and you are probably right. They wear jeans and flannel shirts and ball caps. They drive late-model pick-up trucks, usually big ones with ball hitches for towing. They do not understand why anyone would pay for a service they could do themselves: change the oil in the car, install gutters on the house, build a shed in the backyard.

A lot of them have beards and, more to the point, a lot of the beards are grey. Muzzle loading is a slowly dying sport. Each year, the number of NMLRA members dwindles as older members die off and no new ones fill in behind them. The odds are stacked against these black-powder shooters. More than half of Americans now live in cities. Within a few decades, fewer than half of Americans will be white, and non-whites don't have the same fond memories of the Daniel Boone version of frontier life. The shooters remember the good old days fondly, which helps explain why they shoot rifles using 150-year-old technology.

Each year the shoot sponsors a couple of raffles to raise money. Craftsmen donate genuinely valuable prizes, including rifles worth thousands of dollars. Once I was filling in raffle tickets when I heard an old-timer remark, "I remember the time you could leave a $100 bill on this table, walk off, come back in an hour, and it would still be there. But those days are gone forever, and for the life of me, I don't know why."

I didn't tell him that I had once left my wallet on that same table with more than $600 in it and it was waiting for me when I returned. I didn't tell him because it didn't matter. The world he remembered best— hard working white men making a good living and carrying relatively high social status in their local communities—really was fading, no matter what I said.

I have never conducted formal interviews with the shooters, but I can tell you from hundreds of conversations that most of them are churchgoing Christians who vote Republican. A number of them are Freemasons, as I am myself. Many are U.S. military veterans. A fair number are small business people, but others are union members. They are independent, but in the "God helps those who help themselves" way.

Now that I'm solidly middle-aged myself, I like camping with the shooters because they are generally sober, clean, and quiet. The camp-grounds have playgrounds for the few children (mostly grandchildren) at the shoot. It is not at all uncommon to get dinner invitations. These folks are the solid middle of American society. Some would call them rednecks, but I would simply call them working-to-middle class.

Of all the groups at Friendship, these are people most likely to be sympathetic to the Tea Party insurgency in America. They are concerned about changes underway in their country, but they are deeply invested in America's institutions. They believe in self-reliance, but they are also concerned about social security and Medicare in their retirement. They are concerned about too much government involvement in business and too much wealth redistribution, but they are much too heavily embedded in local government, education, business, and religion to be anarchists of any type. If they protest, they do it as patriots protesting changes they see as overly broad and sweeping expansions of government, biased against individual initiative and hard work.

You may know that almost two-thirds of white working people voted Republican in the 2010 congressional races and these are those people. They feel they have played by the rules: got married, worked hard in a job, stayed married, went to church. They *lose* relative status in a world where resources are transferred from the wealthy to the unemployed, to single parents, or others who in their view have not played by the rules.

Are the shooters alienated? Depends on what you mean. On the one hand, they see themselves as the backbone of true American society. On the other, they see their society changing in ways they find unattractive. And like me, many of them have very consciously, scrupulously avoided becoming organization men, except perhaps for their stints in military service. Many work for themselves as contractors, carpenters, plumbers and mechanics. They grow beards and shoot flintlock rifles. They are the most middle-class of all the groups at Friendship, but even they keep contemporary society at arm's length.

The re-enactors, the folks who camp at Primitive and attend rendezvous all across the U.S., are in one sense a subset of the shooters. They, too, like muzzle loading firearms. But many of them cross some of the boundaries of respectable middle-class life.

I don't want to overplay the difference. Many of the re-enactors are exactly like the shooters except they put more emphasis on the accoutrements—pre-1840 clothes, camp gear, recipes, games, instruments, etc.—and less emphasis, almost by definition, on the technical aspects of shooting. Put another way, a shooter could bore your for hours—literally hours—on the engineering aspects of shooting, whereas a re-enactor would prefer a long argument about whether a particular kind of dinner plate belonged in camp because it was not invented until 1861 and our cut-off date is 1840.

But there is a difference. The folks in Primitive are searching for a lost primal spirit. Their golden era is not the 1950s, but about 1800, on a real frontier. They do not long for a return to working class respectability, but for freedom from it.

You could understand the difference by spending one weekend night at Friendship. On either Friday night, the shooter campgrounds are quiet by 10:00 p.m. Not silent; people sit around the campfire and drink coffee, or even beer. But the emphasis is on conversation. Up in Primitive, there is likely to be live music, heavy drinking by some folks, and carrying on until the small hours of morning. Not by everyone, but by lots of people. I may have witnessed this personally a time or two.

On one Saturday of the shoot, the NMLRA sponsors a barn dance. A bluegrass or country-rock band plays. Although perhaps only 10 percent of the participants at the shoot camp up in Primitive, the Primitive folks dominate the dance. They come dressed in buckskins, in full Seminole regalia, in Revolutionary War costumes. They wear swords and carry carved walking sticks. They drink and dance, sometimes with wild abandon, though as the group ages the abandon recedes. Nowhere is it clearer that although these two groups have closely aligned interests, and although they are more similar to one another than to any groups outside the world of black powder shooting, they are still very different.

Like the shooters, the re-enactors are also staunchly independent. No surprise; people who are trying to blend into middle-American society do not camp in tipis or make their own leather goods or wear pants made from deer hides. But the re-enactors are embedded in a still-smaller subculture. They are part of a community; they have one another. Many make their way on Sunday mornings to the primitive, old-timey church services held on the shooting range. Many hold regular jobs through the year; many others are craftspeople who make and sell their wares to other re-enactors.

They consciously separate themselves from contemporary American life by celebrating a long-gone past. The shooters keep much of current American life at arm's length, but the re-enactors cross the line and stand just slightly outside the system altogether. This is a generalization, of course, and the line is hardly firm, but the re-enactors offer a little louder protest against, and personal subversion of, a world they believe has changed for the worse.

Despite their differences, both the shooters and the re-enactors hold values that I would describe as small town or rural. Most are family people, and in those families the husband has primary responsibility for paid work and the wife primary responsibility for domestic work, including child rearing. They view diversity and pluralism with considerable skepticism. I honestly believe the majority are not racist, if by that one means they harbor a mean-spirited prejudice against people based on skin color or ethnicity. But of course they take a dim view of ethnic separatism or what has been called "black resistance culture." They believe white, middle class values, nuclear families, church attendance, and plain English are the bedrock of American culture. People of other colors and cultural backgrounds are welcome to share in these traditions, but not to challenge them.

The suburbanization of America has led many people to underestimate the difference between urban and rural, but some of the fundamental cleavages in our social structure divide along just such lines. America has a frontier past and a pioneer spirit, neither of which are always visible in a cosmopolitan setting. The frontier and pioneer part of us is rural, but we have always also been a nation of new immigrants living in cities. In the past few decades, we've become a majority-urban nation. This has an enormous effect on our politics, our economic ideas, and even our religion. But we'll get to those as we move through the story of the flea market dealers.

Despite their differences, the shooters and the re-enactors are part of this white, working class culture with small town and rural values. They each "cling"—how the word now resonates—to a different version of a golden age past, but both are right to feel the world shifting under their feet. At the same time, though, the shooters and re-enactors stand near the water's edge of mainstream culture, with the shooters barely in and re-enactors barely out. Virtually all of them have real jobs, though many work for themselves. The large majority are churchgoing Protestants. They vote Republican. Their kids attend public schools. They pay taxes. They keep their money in banks. The big institutions that shape most of our lives shape theirs too, at least to some degree.

Which brings us to the third group, the real subjects of our story: the flea market dealers. Virtually by definition, the dealers live outside the system. They work for themselves. Most of them are not involved in organized religion. During my research project, I pre-selected only those who told me they didn't attend church more than twice per year but, to be honest, such folks are not hard to find in the markets.

Some of the dealers are receiving social security disability benefits or workman's compensation and work in the markets "on the side." Most of the dealers own homes somewhere, but spend much of their time living in tents or trailers out on the road. Their lives are much less directed by the institutions of government, business, or religion that direct most of our lives. They are much less invested in "the system" than either the shooters or even the re-enactors.

The heart of this book is about the dealers and their surprising brand of rugged individualism, but the shooters and the buckskinners make a compelling backdrop because too many people are blind to the difference. The dealers do not just live on the margins of the system, they genuinely distrust it. The shooters and re-enactors might wish things were different, they may even protest in their own ways, but in the end, they are still part of mainstream American culture. The dealers are not; that mainstream may drag them along in its current, but they seem always to be paddling against—or at least beside—it. This is what drew me to them for the formal research on which parts of this book are based. I had experiences and observations and thousands of conversations from twenty years of going to Friendship and I've been to hundreds of flea markets elsewhere, but I wanted some real data grounded in standard interviews. This book uses that research as the axis around which my story and the story of Friendship turns.

To an outsider, Friendship may seem like a "kind" of place. The shooters, re-enactors, flea market dealers, bikers, and even tourists may all seem like a generic segment of white, working class life that can safely be lumped together. But it doesn't seem like that at all from the inside. The shooters consider themselves above the others, even though many would deny it. They are mostly middle class or lower-middle-class people with jobs. They are more likely to attend church, more likely to have been military veterans, less likely to be big drinkers. They can afford thousands of dollars worth of guns and equipment and have sufficient leisure time to use it. Many, as I've pointed out, are now retired. As Friendship goes, this is the ruling class. And besides, they own the shoot grounds and most of the campgrounds. They regulate what goes on within the shoot and charge admission. They are well aware that the flea markets—privately owned property on either side of the shoot itself—benefit from proximity, but they regard the markets as separate and inferior.

I don't know how many shooters have expressed wonder when I said I used to camp at the flea markets, or have advised me to "watch out" for the dealers and the customers. Beyond this, some shooters are even suspicious of the rowdies up in Primitive. They know there is heaving drinking sometimes and suspect there might be drug use.

Even among the shooters there are tight clans. Those who shoot shotguns tend to camp together, as do those who shoot rifles from a bench. There is a separate campground for those who shoot skeet and sporting clays. Even in this very small subculture, there are specialized groups with their own interests and their own social cues from dress to lingo.

The Primitive folks are clannish too. Through the years I have become largely—if perhaps never totally—accepted there because I am very good at one of the prized skills, I volunteer time at the tomahawk range, I always wear Primitive garb while at Friendship, and I donate a fair amount of money. But I don't have a "primitive" camp and am not really one of the tribe. I've heard many Primitive shooters, the re-enactors talk about winning events "across the road," by which they mean in the main part of the shoot. I've heard plenty of shooters complain about unfair and unfriendly treatment by Primitive folks who regarded them as outsiders. I know it seems impossible to believe, but there is tribalism and distrust even among the few thousand NMLRA members who attend the shoots.

Imagine, then, their attitude toward the flea market dealers. Some NMLRA members may wander through the markets, but not as often as you might suppose. Many view the whole thing as a sideshow. The dealers know this—how could they not?—but they also know the shooters and re-enactors have real jobs and cash money. Nothing in muzzle loading or in primitive re-enacting comes cheap.

I have seen the social walls come completely down on only one occasion. When the valley flooded terribly during a shoot in 1996, the three groups pulled together. Honestly, there's always a sense of every man for himself because each is responsible for his own property. But the different groups helped one another because the situation was truly dire. In my interpretation, though, that's just human decency, not a template for later cooperation.

Friendship is a mix of stubborn independence, tired resentment, and a hazy mythology about the past and present. It may sound like what you think of when you think of NASCAR dads or Tea Partiers or militia men. Just how much it's like any of those, though, may become clearer in the pages to follow. And in Friendship, all of this is bound up in America's large and powerful gun culture. A frontier past, the right to bear arms, Live Free or Die: if you don't understand these, you don't understand individualism in America. And if you don't understand individualism—including white male resistance and alienation—at this level of lived culture, you can't really understand America.

3

Cochise, the Dealers,
and the Business World

I WANTED TO TELL the story of the interplay between freedom, religion, and individualism, but there is no way to tell that story—in my experience, no way to tell almost any big story—without considering the role of the marketplace. Since the dealers are, after all, *dealers*, it makes sense to start by understanding the business they are in and considering their attitudes toward business. Living in the country with the biggest, most diverse economy in human history, how did they end up under a plastic tarp selling cut-rate merchandise on a gravel lane 20 miles from anywhere at all and 50 miles from anywhere much?

In my lifetime, junk bonds, savings and loans, and derivatives have all caused capitalist chaos. Flea markets strip buying and selling down to their essence. Someone owns the property where the market takes place. The owner provides retail space, parking, and restrooms. Someone sells food and drink. Individual dealers rent space from the owner and offer merchandise at significant discounts from retail stores. Customers filter through the thousands of items on offer at dozens, maybe hundreds, of individual booths and usually pay cash. Most prices are negotiable; quality varies widely. It's very much like a shopping mall, but with much higher turnover among stores and with face-to-face negotiation over price instead of an endless string of mark-downs from inflated retail. Also, the sellers are almost always independent, never part of a large chain and rarely contractors for a larger seller.

That's the basic framework. But within that is an enormous range of variation not always apparent to tourists and casual shoppers. For instance, there is more than one kind of flea market. The most common is a year-round, stationary market usually housed in abandoned and outdated retail space, but sometimes enclosed in a giant pole-barn built specifically for this purpose. The owner rents out the floor space in small chunks, often 10 by 20 feet. These stationary markets usually open only on the weekend because there is not enough customer traffic to support higher utility costs and the higher rents that come with them, plus some of the dealers work other jobs. Nobody wants to sit at a booth all day if no customers are coming.

Three different kinds of dealers sell in these stationary markets. At the high end are those who specialize in one line of merchandise and are using the flea market as a low-cost point of entry into a straightforward market. For instance, there is likely to be at least one t-shirt shop that does custom design alongside its inventory of pre-made shirts. Frequently one of the booths sells NASCAR paraphernalia exclusively. There may be another that sells wooden signs with names or personal messages routed into them, or another selling metal street signs that say things like "Pacers Fan Parking Only." Knife dealers are common; used gun dealers less so because in many venues, guns mean legal hassles.

The folks who run these booths are small-time entrepreneurs who have made a business decision to "start" in a flea market. They know they would get more traffic in a mall kiosk, but they also know that their rent and their staffing costs would be much higher and they probably don't have the required capital up-front. In the flea market, rent is cheap and they can run their own booth the two or three days it is open each week. They may hope to have their own store some day. You've probably seen t-shirt kiosks and NASCAR stores in shopping malls, and some of those folks may have started in a flea market. People start in the markets because their risk, in terms of time and up-front capital, is very low even if the reward is relatively low too.

These specialist dealers usually have detailed knowledge of the things they sell. Those who make personalized wooden signs or airbrushed t-shirts have a low-level skill which adds to their profits. Some of the specialists are recent immigrants who work for a distributor elsewhere who has staked them to an entry-level retail job as part of a much larger network of people linked by product line and ethnic ties. There are huge networks of African bead dealers who sell some excellent African handicrafts and folk art, though rarely the top of the line saved for art collectors. Frequently there are Chinese dealers selling "everything for a dollar" merchandise out of Tupperware tubs hauled in a box truck from market to market.

You might assume that flea market dealers are not too bright, and it is true that few are college graduates; but some of the specialists are sharp. Some even turn a substantial profit, though it is very hard to say how much because few of them practice true double-entry bookkeeping. They know what price they paid for their goods and what price they need to get for them, but they rarely keep clear, double-entry, records that compare total costs to total receipts, factoring in utilities, labor costs, etc. When a dealer needs to raise cash, things sell cheap. When times are good, prices can be held, unless times are bad for the other guy in the market selling the same stuff. Flea market business is not as rational and precise as big-time retail, but many dealers are able to generate considerable cash flow.

The specialists are the most likely to understand how current, broad trends affect their business. Once, thinking I was pretty smart, I trotted out a theory for a specialist dealer who sold metal signs. "I bet flea markets do better in tough economic times," I offered, "because more people would come here to buy basic items when times are hard." "Nope," he said, "when times get hard for working people they get even harder for me. Nobody's got spare money in their pockets and metal signs are not one of life's necessities. I need customers who have a little money to blow. Worse, when they're laid off from the factory, some of those people think, 'hey, maybe I'll go to work for myself in a flea market.' Then I've got half as many customers and twice as many competitors." I learned to keep my penetrating economic analysis to myself.

The best example of a flea market specialist who can see the big picture is an old friend, the late Trader Bill. For years, he was the man you went to for Griswold, which is the brand name of highly collectible cast-iron skillets and Dutch-ovens. Griswolds are known by shape and size, such as "a Griswold #9." As with any collectible item, value depends on scarcity and condition, including having all the pieces of a set. These add up to what dealers often call "desirability." For instance, if a Dutch oven was originally sold with a trivet and a lid, those accessory pieces by themselves can be quite valuable because there are likely to be many Griswolds of the specific number and size lying around missing their trivets or lids. As with any collectible, having a complete set with all the pieces is the goal.

Like many specialist dealers (especially those who specialize in older items such as pocket knives, guns, coins, or collectible antiques) Trader Bill once made his money by "picking"—going around to yard sales and estate sales buying below wholesale from folks who did not know the value, and then selling to a collector at full retail. Bill knew that collectors were all eager to find that special #9 because it was produced in much smaller quantities than the routine #8 or #10. He would buy pieces at yard sales from people who did not know the difference, or buy whole collections in which he took the bad along with the good, and then make his money selling the rare items at high prices. The coin, knife, and gun markets work much the same way: everyone has the routine stuff and the only way to make a profit is to hold firm on the difference between "buy" and "sell" prices, just like used cars. The only big money is in the odd, rare item that completes a set.

Trader Bill explained to me one day how Ebay changed his business forever. Once Griswold pots and skillets started making their way into online auctions, Bill's margin—the money he made by knowing his field expertly—quickly evaporated. Any novice about to hold a yard sale could go online and find out exactly what a #9 was worth. Any collector could go online and find out what a #9 was selling for. Fewer people sold low or bought high because everyone could see immediately what a fairly rational market would bear.

The online market's ruthless efficiency had an even worse impact on Bill: suddenly #9's were not as rare. People discovered them in their attics and basements; they noticed them when they cleaned out grandma's garage. And they no longer asked themselves, "how in the world would I ever find someone who knows what that's worth?" They knew just where to look.

For consumers, Ebay and other online tools, like Craigslist, is a tremendous benefit because it trims the margin enjoyed by people who have insider expertise. There will always be a difference between "wholesale" and "retail," between what a dealer can pay for an item and what he hopes to sell it for. But the days of making money by having far superior knowledge—what economists call "asymmetrical information"—are fading quickly in the low end world of collectibles just as surely as they have already faded in the high-end world of stocks and bonds. *Most* information about price and value is available quickly and easily to anyone.

Relatively few serious antique dealers set up at flea markets any more. Antique malls offer a similar opportunity to rent a small amount of booth space and they draw a wealthier, which is to say, more fully middle class, clientele. The only reason an antique dealer would choose a flea market is because she specializes in a type of item that would not be attractive to the ordinary antique buyer who is usually looking for home furnishings.

Some people will tell you that this or that flea market "has really gone down hill," by which they mean that it used to have interesting antiques for sale at great prices but now it has a lot of plastic crap from Asia. They are right, of course, but it is not as if the antiques all disappeared. Instead, they went to antique malls and onto Ebay. The power of the marketplace works at the low end just as it does at the high end: it creates levels of specialization that bring buyers and sellers together at the appropriate price point. Antiques have a value separate from, and usually higher than, the items sold at flea markets; inevitably, they wind up in a market of their own and the stuff at flea markets looks more and more like junk because most of it is. This is not a book about the antique market, but if you looked into it you'd see various degrees of specialization there, too, ranging from specialist auctions and interior design shops selling very rare, high-dollar goods right down to small-town antique malls selling what decorators condescendingly call "brown furniture." In the age of Wal-Mart and Ebay, markets shake out quickly, goods and prices find their own level, and true bargains—items bought far below market price—are increasingly rare. Indeed, if you want to find antiques at bargain prices you should be prepared to go to estate sales in hopes of finding items that neither the deceased nor their heirs knew to be valuable—in essence, become your own "picker." (To be fair, the system works both ways. It's now also harder to get ripped off on your own stuff if you do your homework; anyone can learn online roughly how much anything is worth by checking true selling, not asking, prices.)

If the high-end dealer in a stationary flea market usually trades one kind of merchandise, the mid-level dealer sells knick-knacks ranging from very poor quality ceramics to moving, lighted pictures of dolphins or waterfalls to plastic American Indian goods mass produced in

Southeast Asia. The mid-level dealer is a hustler; she sells whatever can be bought cheaply in bulk and sold individually at a significant mark-up.

The range of that mark-up was brought home to me when my dad got laid off and started selling in markets. He wanted to make money trading guns, but that can only be done by buying at wholesale and selling at retail, and almost everyone with one gun to sell or trade knows the retail price and is willing to wait until he finds a buyer. The gun market has been rationalized for years, even before Ebay, through printed price guides. Dad also hoped to make money trading antiques but the same problem applies: the dealer must either acquire them at wholesale market value or find a client who is willing to pay above ordinary retail for just the right piece. Both strategies are labor intensive. (That is, after all, how antique dealers make money in interior design. They don't have to buy so low if they know they can sell high to people with specific decorating desires and plenty of money—they're not getting paid for the antique piece, they are getting paid for their skill in identifying and acquiring it.)

Even in his part-time flea market dealing, Dad found quickly that there was money in knick-knacks. In the 1980s, small, fake-turquoise, fake-silver, rings were very popular. They sold for $1.00 apiece. I was stunned to find that Dad could buy them wholesale at $3.00 per 100. Other knick-knacks had similar mark ups. Cheap imports from Asia were filtering down past the discount department stores to the flea market dealers who bought in much smaller quantities. They had to pay a little more for their goods since they bought fewer at a time, but they had much, much less overhead and so could compete on price.

The problem, however, will be obvious to anyone who has ever worked retail: when the same imported goods are available to everyone, it is impossible to keep prices up. Some dealer will change her mind and decide to go out of business. Or she'll really need money for that week's rent. In either case, she's willing to sell her fake-turquoise rings for 75 cents. Or 50 cents. Suddenly the bottom is out of the market.

That's the bad news, but the good news is not real good either. Even if the price holds up and each ring brings the full $1.00 for a 3000 percent profit, at the end of the day if you sell a whole bag of 100 rings you still only made $97.00. So the mid-level knick-knack dealers shift from novelty item to novelty item just trying to keep enough cash flow to pay the bills and move on to the next potential big money maker. My dad sold trinkets to cover his booth rental, which included camping fees, so he could trade the guns and antiques that he loved but could not make much money with.

At the bottom of the flea market hierarchy, especially in stationary markets, is the junk dealer. Even if most flea market stuff is junk, this junk still defines the field. Junk dealers buy boxes at yard sales, odd lots at auctions, and the unsold remainders of estates. They pick up items set out with the trash in affluent neighborhoods. They bring them to their booth to see if anyone will make a cash offer.

When this strategy works—and frequently it does not—it is because dealers acquire re-saleable goods so incredibly cheaply. A friend of mine who trades guns in his booth pays his expenses in just this way. He cannot pass a yard sale without stopping. If something seems cheap and useful, he buys it. The seller is happy to get rid of something she would otherwise have thrown away, so it does not matter if a used hedge trimmer worth $20 sells for $2, because $2 is better than nothing. My friend buys it, throws it in a trailer, then sets it out on his table, across from the guns, at the flea market. He does not expect to get the $20 value either. But if he gets $10, or even $5, he makes a little money for almost no work.

You may be wondering: does he really make money if you count the gas, the time he spent at yard sales, and the time and resources necessary to set up his booth? Who knows? He doesn't keep books with all that information and doesn't care. Fact is, he likes yard sales and he likes setting up in flea markets and gun shows, so if this creates some spare cash on rent day, he can live with it.

Very few get rich trading junk, but some people make a bare living. For others, it's a way to generate enough cash flow to mitigate the risk out of trading the goods that really interest them. For many, it is a desperate way to earn pocket money to subsidize their disability check or other basic, often subsistence-level, income.

Central Indiana has several stationary, year-round, flea markets. I've been to dozens of them, but I conducted my interviews at Circle City flea market on the south side of Indianapolis. Circle City, like the area that surrounds it, is full of white working-class people, many of whose families moved to Indiana from West Virginia and Kentucky. A nearby neighborhood is, in fact, called "Little Kentucky." If you're from New York or Los Angeles you'll likely find it hilarious that Hoosiers look down on neighboring states they consider backward and rustic, but it is true.

Like the neighborhood, this south side flea market has a growing population of Chinese and Hispanic immigrants, both as dealers and customers. In central Indiana, working-class Asians and Hispanics, especially those from Mexico, continue to move into poor white neighborhoods rather than poor black ones.

Circle City is housed in an abandoned K-Mart. The paint is weathered and worn and the parking lot full of potholes, but the lights and the plumbing work. It is open Friday, Saturday, and Sunday year round, but many of the booths are closed Fridays because their owners are working other jobs while waiting for their flea market business to grow. The fluorescent tube lights very high above the floor give the whole place a kind of washed, pallid look. An awful lot of what is sold there is junk, but there are some old pocket knives and used computers. (Old computers, oddly enough, occasionally sell for more than they are worth at flea markets because buyers unfamiliar with them do not realize that they are worth essentially nothing, though this mistake is made by fewer and fewer people each year.)

Circle City operates year round and, in fact, does a brisk Christmas business, but many stationary markets are seasonal. Seasonal markets are often held outdoors, sometimes in conjunction with some kind of tourist attraction, sometimes in rural areas where retail shopping is limited. Many of these markets are set under corrugated metal roofs with open sides. I conducted interviews in three such markets in Gnawbone, Indiana, which is located on Indiana Highway 46, the main road from Interstate 65 into Brown County, where the tourists come to experience old-time, small-town, rural Indiana in the summer and fall. It is really the only place in Indiana that gets "leaf peepers" and many of them are willing to pay good money for fudge or apple butter for their fried biscuits to complete the experience. If you've ever been to Gatlinburg or Branson, you can imagine Brown County, Indiana, and its county seat, Nashville, as scaled-down versions. There was even a "Little Nashville Opry" where nationally-known country music acts that are not quite at the top, or just past it, performed during the tourist season, but sadly the Little Opry burned down during the time I have worked on this book.

There is no traffic light or stop sign, so you don't technically have to slow down for Gnawbone, but it is a good idea to do so because so many cars leave and enter the highway. The old Marathon station sold deep-fried pork tenderloins that were once featured on *Good Morning America,* but the station's closed now. A small country store sells baked goods, candy, and outdoor flowers. In the fall, their mums are both cheap and spectacular. Two of the three flea markets have permanent structures, essentially pole barns with metal roofs. The largest market has a campground, a pay fishing lake, and two buildings in which the booths are fully enclosed. This big market has many regular vendors, including specialists who sell collectible pins, ceramics, candles, and other items at a discount to mall retail.

The smallest and best of the three markets, Gypsy Moon, is really only a gravel parking lot with metal pole frames. The dealers stretch plastic tarps across these to protect their goods. Most of the booths sell used furnishings and worn items bought at yard sales. There are some antiques, which is to say some of the junk is old, but not the Louis XIV kind sold at Sothebys.

Beyond the stationary and seasonal markets are my favorites, the markets that set up in conjunction with big events. Anywhere a crowd of working people is likely to gather there will be a market. If there's a gathering where people are willing to eat fried pork rinds—from the National Coon Dog Trials in Kenton, Ohio to the Covered Bridge Festival in Rockville, Indiana—there will be flea markets that are often a bigger draw than the event they grew up around.

I've spent many years in the two markets of this kind of surrounding Friendship. The markets are clearly distinct, with one on each side of the shoot. The one attached to the town of Friendship itself is called the Old Mill. It's really just a big, gravel lot that runs from town down to the creek. Attached to it, running away from town, is a large field where literally thousands are camped during the four weekends of the two annual shoots. The bigger of the two markets, about one mile from town on the other side of the shoot, is Tom Kerr's. Actually, its official name is the Friendship Flea Market, but it is *always* called after its owner. Ask someone where she bought an item she is carrying and she will say "I got it up at Old Mill" or "it came from over at Tom Kerr's"; everyone knows what she means.

Both markets are full of regulars. As I mentioned, I've been to at least one of the two shoots in twenty-four out of the last twenty-five years, and I've met dealers who have been to both shoots for more than forty years running. Sometimes business is bad, sometimes it is good, and often it's fair to middling. The items on offer change slowly. Twenty years ago there were no compact discs or fiber optic signs. And the antiques really have gradually migrated out to the antique malls, so the complaints that "there used to be better stuff" are not merely nostalgic.

The Friendship markets have a lot of specialty items specific to the occasion. The kind of people who come as tourists to the muzzle loading championships like to imagine themselves as outdoorsy, so Friendship is full of dealers selling knives, guns, and army surplus. You may have wondered about the guns. In general, any adult can sell long guns—rifles and shotguns—without much hassle from law enforcement. Pistols— other than muzzle loading, black powder pistols—are prohibited. I'm sure many people at Friendship are carrying loaded pistols, .38s and .45s, they think of as "personal protection," but these are not legally sold, traded, or even shown in the markets. You rarely see a pistol, other than black-powder pistols, at Friendship.

Some of my urban friends are stunned to find that guns change hands so easily, but neither the state police nor the market owners have any special reason to discourage this. They're just guns. This is a shooting event, so the huge majority of the people here already own firearms. The ones for sale in the market are not concealable. They are used for hunting or target shooting or, in many cases, for placing in a gun case and showing off to friends. Dozens of guns change hands every day in Friendship and literally thousands of rounds are fired, though nearly every one of these is front-loaded with black powder. I'm sure there have been unintended explosions, but in twenty-five years I don't know of a single shooting of a person, intentional or accidental.

In addition to the outdoor equipment, there are many items associated with the eighteenth- and early nineteenth-century frontier. These are what make Friendship what it is. If you make or sell leather work, beadwork, moccasins, tomahawks, or furs, Friendship is an excellent market. Thousands of tourists come here because of their interest in antique firearms and frontier life; how often will you get a better target audience? I know one dealer, a fur trapper, who drives with his son to Friendship from Montana each year. He has even purchased a small log cabin, which he keeps on wheels, to use as his shop while he's in town. Tourists love a log cabin.

The "frontier" goods run the gamut. Many of these are sold within the confines of the shoot itself, where dealers may only display items that are fully in the spirit of the enterprise. The tin-roofed sheds within the shoot are not really a flea market at all; there is no cheap plastic crap. And the shooters who own $4000 rifles are not hesitant to pay good money for the other accoutrements. A carved powder horn can cost hundreds. My own buckskin trousers cost $200. My Paul Poppen moccasins cost about $150. Until I bought a pair of Church's dress shoes while living in England, my moccasins were the most expensive shoes I'd ever owned. Some clothiers in the shoot make a living selling fabric, patterns, and clothes they have made themselves, usually from linen or wool. Rents are higher for dealers in the shoot, but they can focus on their very specific clientele and charge prices that reflect their level of craftsmanship and expertise.

Some of the frontier trade does make its way over into the two flea markets. There are, for instance, some less expensive, but still hand-made, moccasins for sale at Old Mill. The fur trader from Montana is in the flea markets, as are several leather dealers. I know one couple who own a successful leather shop in Louisville but bring their odd lots and end pieces to Friendship because there is a built-in market for useful scraps and weathered hides. Those who trade in beads and arrowheads can be found in the flea markets as well as at the shoot.

The bead trade is beyond me. The fanatics think nothing of spending hundreds of dollars for just the right glass beads. Old Indian beads—the genuine article—are extremely valuable. Large beads are made into elaborate necklaces; even more impressive, tiny beads are carefully sewn into patterns on buckskin, especially onto moccasins and knife sheaths. Contemporary glass artisan Art Seymour always makes it to Friendship, where his multi-layered, large, beads can bring a thousand dollars each. Even more spectacular than the beads can be the quillwork, in which porcupine quills are sliced thin, dyed, and then threaded into buckskin or leather. This is obviously tedious work and prices for the good stuff are high, but good quillwork is worn as a status symbol.

Even though high-end rifles may sell for thousands, they contain hundreds of dollars worth of materials and dozens of hours of expert labor. The biggest profit at Friendship is made not by the gun makers but by the food vendors. The shoot has a cafeteria run by a local restaurant, but both flea markets have carnival food vendors who set up for both nine-day sessions.

The type of food is no surprise. There are elephant ears, bar-b-q, ribeye steak sandwiches, Buffalo burgers, corn on the cob, pork rinds, and fried walleyed pike. The biggest money is made at the soft-serve ice cream booth. The two owners are on their feet 10 to 12 hours per day filling and serving one size of cone for $1.50. The food market is so lucrative that the vendors must not only pay extra rent but, in one of the markets, must also pay a percentage of their daily profit. In exchange for these higher costs, they get a protected monopoly. Tom Kerr allows only one ice cream stand and it always sits right at the front of the market nearest the highway; it is impossible not to walk past it on the way in and out.

Food would, of course, be available at any market of any size. Junk and cheap Asian goods are also everywhere. Neither of these are what brings the tourists. Honestly, the shooting events themselves are not the main draw either. After all, what do you really see when you watch shooting? A man holds a gun and fires it at a paper target too distant to be seen clearly. Occasionally a specialty event is worth watching, like when the buckskinners split a ball off an axe blade to break two clay pigeons, but even that gets old quickly. Either they can do it or they can't and after watching a couple of tries the kids are ready to go get ice cream.

No, the tourists are drawn by the spectacle of frontiersmen wearing buckskin pants and hats made from whole animal skins—some with head and teeth still attached. They are drawn by the coyote pelts and tomahawks and arrowheads for sale. They are drawn by the sheer size of the flea markets and the possibility that they'll find something cheap or interesting or at least distracting. If there's a redneck truism on a t-shirt—including anything Larry the Cable Guy ever said—it will be for sale at Friendship. My favorite t-shirt says, "I'd Rather Be Historically Accurate Than Politically Correct."

And what draws the dealers? The obvious answer is the customers. But many of the dealers come back to both shoots, year after year, even when business has been consistently slow. Friendship *is* a rendezvous, a place where like-minded people gather for a combination firearm convention and swap meet.

The buckskinners—the re-enactors—would scoff at the notion of Friendship as a rendezvous. When they say "rendezvous," they mean a meeting of other buckskinners where pre-1840 standards for dress and equipment will be enforced much more rigorously than they are at Friendship. Rendezvous like those are held throughout the country during the warm months; some of them contain thousands of campsites. For those most serious rendezvous-ers, Friendship is a circus in which they are the sideshow.

But Friendship is a rendezvous in its own right, a ritual gathering that is performed with eerie precision year after year. The shooting events happen on the same days. The dealers return to their same spots. But more than any of this, each night when the sun goes down, the live entertainment at the flea markets emerges as a carbon copy of years past.

This is no exaggeration. In the twenty-five years I've been at Friendship, the same band—Dale Hill and the Whiskey River Band—has appeared nightly in the red barn at the Tom Kerr market. They play the whole spectrum of music, from Hank Williams to Hank Williams Jr. ("We have both kinds, country and western.") In the past decade, the music has been rocked-up a little to suit the younger crowd. They have drums, separating them from bluegrass, and now they do a few rock standards from artists like Bob Seger or the Eagles.

Their stage paints the picture vividly. It is draped with more than twenty Confederate flags, including an 8 feet by 10 feet one right behind the band. When the sun goes down and the tourists go home, many of the dealers make their way up to the small barn. The band stays inside the barn with the door rolled open (they can roll the door closed at 1:00 a.m. to store their equipment over night and to leave the flags in place between shoots). The audience stands or sits in lawn chairs around a large concrete circle meant for dancing. In the center of the circle is a very large bonfire—some nights it is huge, fueled with dozens of wooden pallets. Once you have been to a Dale Hill bonfire, it is hard to think of Friendship without the image of peering through flames and smoke, beer in hand, watching flea market vendors two-stepping as an aging man with a yellowed beard and weathered cowboy hat sings "Your Cheatin' Heart." The Indiana State Police sometimes wander through the bystanders to make sure there is no underage drinking or blatant use of controlled substances. There are both, of course, but at least the cops make sure things don't get too out of hand.

Things are much tamer at the Old Mill which is, after all, right in town. The Old Mill's owner lives right in Friendship himself. There, dealers who play various instruments gather inside the meeting hall to join in on slow, mournful versions of old country and gospel standards. At some point, a heavy-set woman in a funny hat will sing "You Are My Sunshine." There is free popcorn. People sit respectfully, often clapping and singing along. If you've already been to see Dale Hill up at Tom Kerr's, the Old Mill seems like the Lawrence Welk Show. It is what Friendship would look like if all of it was designed by Southern Baptists.

This is the official entertainment, but there is a lot of impromptu music too. At flea market booths where guitars and banjos are sold, pickers sometimes gather in the early evening. Two of my best friends, Dan and Shane, are accomplished bluegrass players—paid professionals, though not full time—who wander like minstrels to different large campfire gatherings. One of the great benefits of sitting at our little campfire is that other wandering musicians will stop by looking for Dan and Shane.

One fellow who sounds remarkably like Elvis plays guitar and sings to a karaoke background track from his flea market booth in the early evenings—he even sells CDs of himself singing. Two members of Dale Hill's band set up folding tables in the Tom Kerr market during the day and play guitar in hopes of selling a few of their own CDs.

When there's no music, people hang around the hundreds of campfires and tell stories. They come back to Friendship twice a year and sit with the same friends, listen to the same Dale Hill music drifting through the background, and tell the same lies and tales of adventure they told last year. And drink beer.

These people, the dealers working the markets, drinking beer, and listening to country music draped in rebel flags, are the subjects of my interviews, the reason I wrote this book. I interviewed at the Circle City flea markets and in Gnawbone to make sure I was getting the story right, but the foundation for my observations and conversations was always Friendship.

My observations and experiences through the years set me up to write this book, but it's not only about my general impressions. I designed a research project in which I interviewed sixty dealers at the flea markets in Circle City, Gnawbone, and Friendship.

I walked the flea markets telling dealers about my project and asking if they'd be interested in talking to me. Because the Friendship flea markets run ten days—from Friday until the following Sunday—

I tried to catch the dealers there during mid-week when they were not so busy. I visited Circle City on Fridays because Saturdays and Sundays are busier. The Gnawbone markets are only open on the weekend, so I tried to show up early—say 9:00 a.m.—before the tourists came. I paid $20 cash on the spot for an interview that averaged about 45 minutes. I took handwritten notes but also tape-recorded each interview for later transcription. I asked each respondent to sign a waiver giving me permission to use the content of their interview with the understanding that no one would be identified in whatever I produced. You won't be surprised to learn that most of my respondents said they'd be happy to be identified. Most commonly they told me what they thought and added "and I don't care who knows it." I was doing this project on my own with funding given to me as an individual, so I wasn't bound by university rules, but I could not help but be cautious about any possible ill effects to what social scientists call "human subjects," especially since several of these particular humans were friends of mine.

My response rate was overwhelmingly positive; very few people said "no thanks." This made it much easier to try to get a mix of men and women and a broad cross-section of age groups. Friendship was a great place to conduct the research because I already had many contacts. Not only were some of those people willing to talk to me themselves, but they were willing to vouch for me with their friends and associates whom I did not know. I had to work a little harder at Circle City and Gnawbone to gain trust. At Circle City, I lucked into an early interview with a wonderful woman who took a liking to me and introduced me to her friends (did I mention the $20?). At Gnawbone I had to work table by table. As you'll see in the chapters to come, flea market dealers are a distrustful bunch, so sometimes I had to do a fair amount of explaining.

In consultation with several of my university colleagues, I established a fixed set of questions which I asked in every interview. From time to time I would change the order of the questions a little because I sensed a natural segue or because a previous answer made a question irrelevant. But in general, I got parallel responses because I repeatedly asked the same questions. This was not like a survey, though. I had the ability to probe and push when the opportunity presented itself. I could see themes that I thought were worth pursuing; occasionally, I could see when we weren't getting anywhere and then try to change course.

Before moving to the interviews, though, we should take just a moment to reflect on flea markets as a form of human activity. I believe flea markets shed some light on the enormous, transformative power of capitalism, the degree to which capitalism creates individualism, and the ways in which individualism plays out all too often as consumerism.

The power of capitalism is so overwhelming that it hardly needs me to note it. It is true that the huge bureaucratic state, most clearly embodied in the U.S. federal government, is also strong and pervasive, but even it can be bent to the will of the market. If you don't think so, ask yourself which power won in the *former* Soviet Union: the Soviet state machine or global capitalism? Ask yourself which will ultimately win in China? In India? Most people want a better material life. They will re-arrange their activities to achieve it. I don't see how anyone looking at the global marketplace could think otherwise.

Flea markets *are* capitalism in action because they are face-to-face markets where prices are negotiated through direct conversation. But that's only the most basic link between flea markets and a capitalist economy. Flea markets are a testament to the ways capitalism creates a particular brand of individualism. This is the entry level for people who do not want to be, or could not cut it as, organization men (or women). This is where you get to work for yourself, where you can wear your hair as wish, where nobody tells you what to do.

Who shops in flea markets? People looking for a bargain, people who often feel ordinary retail outlets take too much profit; people who think they can beat the price system by cutting out the middle men. And of course, people with a little disposable income who see shopping as entertainment, the way all those Americans flocking to malls do.

Who sells in flea markets? People who do not work in the regular system; people who do not want to listen to a boss or punch the clock; people have taken direct, personal responsibility—willingly or not—for their own economic future. Flea market dealers are often old hippies or rednecks who could not stand the authority inherent in working for a larger organization. Or they are former manufacturing employees who are now on Social Security disability benefits and are trying to supplement their income on the side. (The degree to which this is legal is none of my business here.) Or they got fired for misconduct or poor performance. Both buyers and sellers define themselves as solitary actors managing their own interests; both are trying to gain a small advantage by working on the margins of the system.

Relatively little regulation applies. Flea market dealers sell used firearms, pornographic DVDs, perfume, and animal parts used for clothing and decoration (though at Friendship, the government does regulate the sale of certain animal parts, at least when the Conservation Officers are on the grounds). Caveat emptor obtains across the board. Cash is the currency, and a deal is a deal.

In other societies—say, the former Soviet Union—a flea market might be considered a "black market" because it undermined political regulation of prices by letting the market run solely on supply and demand. But in the U.S., "black market" would only apply if narcotics, automatic weapons, or something else illegal to own was being traded. Otherwise, flea markets are just the lowest, most direct form of retail. In a trickle down economy, this is where goods—both cheap new imports and used debris—trickle down to.

It might be fair to call it a "gray market," however, because of the dubious tax situation. The state excise tax officers come through the markets at least once a shoot to make sure the dealers have their tax ID numbers and have paid their registration. Beyond this, though, it would cost more to enforce the collection of sales tax than the value of the tax being collected, so it rarely happens.

Because regulation is light, capitalism is exercised in a pure form, and both buyers and sellers act as free agents, you might think flea markets would be impossible to describe or predict since literally anything goes. But in fact flea markets are fairly routine and surprisingly predictable, which is why I've been able to summarize them here.

They are predictable because consumer tastes are predictable, despite the individualism of each buyer and seller. Flea markets sell practical items—tools and clothes—to people who either cannot or will not pay the higher price associated with name brands. True, it is harder to return a faulty item for refund. So consumers who are willing or forced to pay less take their chances.

But beyond the practical items, flea markets offer pop culture at a discount. They sell t-shirts with NASCAR drivers or the latest clever catch-phrase. ("Git 'er done" has had its day, but what a day it was.) They sell useless crystal balls and ornate swords with dragon-head handles to the young people who watched *Buffy the Vampire Slayer* or now read the myriad vampire and gothic teen books. They sell discount pocket knives and fishing tackle to men who like to imagine they'll spend more time outdoors than they really ever will. (Hint: they'll actually be at work or in front of the television dreaming of more stuff to buy.) They sell old junk to people who imagine they are collecting antiques, perhaps with an eye to the item's future price appreciation.

Flea markets cater to consumers the same way malls do—they supply the materials for a kind of individual consumerism that is socially constructed and managed through advertising. Just as Hollister and Abercrombie and Fitch deliver the style for a particular segment of "lifestyle choice," flea markets do much the same in a very different segment. Buying and selling may be capitalism, but "shopping" is entertainment.

While it is true that the social foment of the 1960s destroyed the imagined homogeneity of white, middle-class culture in America, what arose was not a new culture, the hippie dream of communalism, ecological awareness, and greater shared social responsibility. What really rose from the ashes of the 60s was greater individual consumer choice with an emphasis on personal expression. Capitalism rode that wave onto the beaches of consumerism and commercialism, channeling expression into lifestyle choices such as preppy, corporate, outdoorsy, gay/urbane, and the like. On the edges were lifestyles like Harley, Goth, or punk.

Don't get me wrong; I'm neither romantic about nor highly critical of this lifestyle-choosing, consumer-driven individualism. What people *can* choose is constrained by the state and the market; what they wish to choose is shaped by their upbringing, their environment, by music, by magazines, and mostly by television. But it's pointless to say that what came out of the 60s is a new corporatism or a new liberalism or a neo-conservatism or anything else. What came out of the 60s is ALL of that as personal culture was fragmented into millions of different combinations of consumer choice.

In many ways, public culture got *more* homogeneous. The commercial area of any city looks the same: McDonalds, Walmart, Home Depot, etc. The content of the painting is the same, but we each build our own special lenses through which we see it.

Flea markets do not merely provide cheap goods, they provide the material for those who either chose an independent lifestyle or simply find themselves odd-man-out in the big game of mass culture lifestyle sorting. Flea markets are full of people—both buyers and sellers—who are individualists by choice or by default, folks on the margin of an economic and political system that is far beyond their control. The best they can hope for is to beat the system occasionally or to limit, even symbolically, its ability to control them.

Don't ever underestimate the desire by individuals to limit external, especially systemic, control. Selling in a flea market is not about making more money than in a real job in a factory, it's about being out from under the thumb of a boss. Gun fanaticism is rarely about shooting, usually about freedom from government control and the ability to protect one's autonomy. A redneck's home is his castle because he can defend it. At the most basic, personal level, the system cannot force an armed man to do what he refuses to do. You can talk all you want about how someone's political choices, consumerist attitudes, and slavery to pop culture are shaped by forces far beyond their control, but there is a bottom line at which my freedom to trade with whom I choose, for cash, and my ability to separate myself from the government and from others because I am armed, gives me a kind of freedom. It may not be your kind of freedom, but the idea that it's somehow not real is gravely mistaken.

Cochise in the Market

"I don't understand the growth economy," Cochise admitted. "I don't understand why everything has to keep getting bigger: take more money, develop more land, more, more, more. I guess maybe I'm a minimalist. I just don't think I need more than I really need."

You would never mistake Cochise for one of the anarchists or other anti-globalization protestors who would occasionally break the windows out of a London McDonald's during a pathetic little riot. In fact, Cochise says he believes in capitalism, just as he believes in a strong work ethic and personal responsibility. He regards those as worthy ideals. In practice, he sees business people, mostly corporate executives, who use their power to stick it to people like him.

"On a higher level, and here I'm talking about big corporations and their rich boards of directors, it is ruthless and immoral. In the end, the employees, hell, even the customers are just pieces in a puzzle, just component parts as the companies decide how to squeeze the last dime out of every single thing they do."

"When I worked for the company," Cochise would say, "I was just amazed by their whole philosophy and attitude. I would assume if that big corporation was that way, which is so much a part of America, then that mentality and that mindset goes through all the businesses they touch."

"What is that mindset?" I pressed. "What is it about it that disturbs you?"

"The profit, the amount of profit they have to have at whatever expense it is, whether it's the human expense, the environmental expense."

"I've got a buddy," he went on, "whose father was a corporate vice president and he worked for a gentleman with incredible ethics. He took great care of the people who worked for him and was a marvelous man. But those guys don't exist any more. Unions tried to get in his shop forever and could never do it because the employees were so happy with their situation. But you couldn't do that today. The corporate world chews people up and spits them out."

Cochise sees ruthless efficiency and an alliance between big business and government as two sides of the same coin. In both cases they're squeezing the little guy, the small business owner. When economists think of small businesses they may be thinking in terms of dozens, or a few hundred, employees. But Cochise means independent entrepreneurs in business for themselves. Everything is stacked against them: taxes, outsourcing, immigration, banking, insurance and, of course, Wal-Mart. It's all set up to benefit the people who already have the power and money. It takes business from the little guy or blocks his entry altogether.

The myth about taxes is as strong as the myth of welfare. Flea market dealers are convinced that the rich avoid taxes and the middle class—by which they mean themselves—get stuck with the bill. Because my wife spent three years as vice-president in a Fortune 500 company, I tend to think differently about taxes. I know we paid many, many times as much in taxes as most of my dealer friends make. But the received wisdom is that the rich get tax breaks and get off the hook. If you have ever listened to conservative talk show host Rush Limbaugh, you'll know that this is one of his pet peeves. He wants working people to understand that the rich pay virtually all taxes. His website has a permanent feature showing that the top 50 percent of income earners pay about 97 percent of all taxes, with the top 1 percent paying 38 percent by themselves. He knows what is said, and believed, out in the working world where people distrust the poor who receive assistance and the wealthy who receive subsidies.

Those same folks also distrust new immigrants or, more precisely, distrust the policies that seem to rush new immigrants into the work-place. Few flea market dealers I spoke with had any personal disregard for the Spanish-speakers, mostly Mexican, who have recently come to Indiana in large numbers. There are stories of drunkenness and violence, to be sure, but I know this has been true for all working-class immigrant groups through the decades. I was way more likely to hear the dealers say: "I'll give them this, though, those people work hard."

It's common to hear a dealer say, "I don't blame the Mexicans. Hell, I'd come here too if I thought I could make more money. But for the life of me I don't understand why our country lets them take our jobs, not pay taxes, and not have to learn English." The language barrier is especially grating. Even people who want to be tolerant when it comes to economic necessity cannot stand the thought of being asked to speak or understand Spanish in their own country. On this score, simple polite-ness often breaks down.

Outsourcing is seen as the other side of the same coin. I remem-ber discussing the Six Sigma projects at my wife's work with one of my Friendship pals. Six Sigma, as you may know, is a problem-solving process that emphasizes cost cutting and other time or energy savings meant to produce ever greater efficiency. Said my friend, "Yeah, my wife was learning that too. Sounds to me like it should be called 'Let's Do Everything as Fast as We Can and as Cheap as We Can No Matter How Many Jobs We Ship to Mexico.'" My wife didn't think her company would be willing to change the program name.

Ross Perot was right on the money when he thought many working people would oppose NAFTA—remember "that giant sucking sound"? But there are not enough disgruntled individualists like the flea market dealers to champion that agenda and folks like the flea market dealers are unlikely to vote. If many of the people who are most unhappy with trade policy are also the least likely to be organized or to get involved in politics, then pro-business policies are a safe political position. After all, if there is no difference between Republicans and Democrats when it comes to coziness with big money—and the dealers sure don't see any big differences—then it does not make sense to waste a lot of time on the outcome.

Cochise considers current trade policy, especially exporting labor jobs overseas, short-sighted. "If you don't have anybody making a decent wage, they can't spend money. At some point they are going to run out of people spending money. That's what it amounts to."

He went on, "We need to change taxes on import goods, export goods, stop sending all the jobs across the seas for cheap labor. They just allow our corporations and companies here to move. I mean just move for profit. Not move for need, move for profit. I mean, I could understand if the material was there, but we are taking the material from here and putting it together there and bringing it back here. Strictly profit. We have the bulk of what we need here to survive in America."

In Cochise's world, the people who buy things are people like himself. They are going to be unemployed, out of money, and unable to consume. It would be hard for him to understand how far down the scale he really is, how little his consumption matters. I believe he is right about Americans running out of money to consume because of a shifting labor market. Unfortunately, he is only right about a relatively small percentage of Americans and they are going to have to bear the burden more or less alone.

No corporate interests are immune from the cynicism and distrust. Cochise is a lifelong smoker, but he still thinks the tobacco companies are pulling the strings. "You cannot get rid of cigarettes because this country was founded on tobacco. That's all there is to it. What's running our politics is money, and tobacco companies are big in it, big, big, big. And like most businesses, they are shipping out. You know what I mean, going out of country."

Perhaps the oddest case is Wal-Mart. It is no secret that working people shop at Wal Mart because selection is high and prices are low. Comedians tell stock jokes about working couples having a "night out" shopping at the Wal-Mart. The giant retailer once had a reputation for buying American-made whenever they could. But now Wal-Mart competes solely on price and many of its goods come from outside the U.S. On top of this, the company has recently battled claims that it underpays workers and withholds benefits.

Most of the dealers admit shopping there, of course, because they buy on price and convenience as most people do. But they are not unaware that Wal-Mart is another multinational corporation making it difficult for small businesses. The dealers are less concerned with the kind of Main Street shops that struggle to compete because they are less rooted in any particular small town community, but they still see Wal-Mart as a piece in the same puzzle. (To be clear: the more rooted you are in your hometown and the way you imagine it's always been, the more skeptical you are of Wal-Mart's contributions.)

Cochise put it like this: "I do shop there some only because I have to because it is so inexpensive. But they run everybody else out. They run the small man out and they get a lot of labor from China, which is prison labor, and child labor, and I just don't believe in that. I have also heard they are a very fundamentalist family and that don't really ride. I mean, I believe everybody has the right to their religious belief, but there are some religions that you know it is either their way or you are going to burn in hell, so it don't matter, and those types I just try to steer clear of."

You might assume—as I did—that people like Cochise blame lawyers for many of the world's woes, just as the middle class does—or at least did, before people switched to bankers as the bogeymen. But probe as I might, I could barely get a mention of lawyers from any of my respondents. Even the ones who had been involved in disability suits don't see lawyers as the problem. I directly asked the question, "Are there any kind of businesses or professions you distrust, anyone with whom you prefer not to do business?" Lawyers never come up.

Insurance companies, however, are a different story. People told me over and over that they had been treated unfairly by insurance companies and, more surprising still, banks. I think of these two institutions as cumbersome but value-neutral; that's not how Cochise and the others see it.

"I don't like insurance. I think that it, in a big way, is a rip off. I think the American public could in a more easily organize-able fashion make the same amount of money on their own if they were just taught to, and I think that insurance takes advantage of this. I mean, you can't live without it. You have to have it. If you don't have it, sooner or later you're going to be stuck with a bill you can't pay. I would say that is my biggest distrust. Not having insurance is not a luxury I can afford. The insurance industry may be screwed, but they've got me screwed too."

Most dealers do not have liability insurance that covers their booths, though a few do. The markets themselves carry liability insurance, of course. But liability is not the only issue. Unless they are retired from regular jobs, they dealers tend not to have any health or medical insurance either. They are on their own in more ways than one.

It is no trick to understand why flea market dealers distrust insurance companies. Many of the dealers feel they got a raw deal in a former disability action. And they are much more likely to blame the insurance companies than the lawyers. They find insurance a kind of blackmail, a protection they cannot afford to buy and also cannot afford to be without. The insurance companies ask lots of nosy questions. And most of the time, you pay money in and get nothing back. Nothing about the insurance business is designed in a flea market dealer's favor.

It's a little harder to figure why the dealers dislike banks, but over and over I heard stories of people who had money go missing or some similarly bad experience. Cochise summed it up: "I have known plenty of people who have had their accounts tampered with and money withdrawn by other family members and their money came up missing and the bank don't know why. In the end, it ain't worth it. You never know from one minute to the next if that bargain is there and it will just get right past you and you will never survive doing it. Sometimes you need a $100, sometimes you might need $10 or something like that, so I just keep it rolling all the time. Nobody takes checks for a good deal. Cash has to be on hand at all times."

Overhearing this piece of our conversation, the lady at the booth next to him said, "I don't like dealing with banks. I really don't because I have had so many problems with them. Like me and my sister both have accounts at the bank, same bank, and they put my money in her bank account and I went to get money out of the bank and they told me I didn't have what I had in there. I asked and said well, I put it in there last week. They said well, we will have to check into it, and they found out they had put it in my sister's account. And then, my niece—my nephew's wife, me and her are about the same size and we used to live in their house before we moved out. And we had our bank checks come to their house and she went and got our checks and got my money out of the bank there, too. They let her have my money, so now I don't have no bank account. I keep my money at home. I don't have nothing to do with banks anymore."

Of the big three social forces in this analysis—business, religion, politics—I would say the dealers' distrust for business was the weakest because business people were more transparent, at least, than religious people and not as frighteningly coercive as the government. Business people cannot, as a rule, force you to buy things from them or put you in jail for ignoring them. And you know what they want: to make money. Asked flatly whether they trust other businesses and believe financial matters are conducted fairly in the U.S., more than half of my respondents said "no" and only a third said "yes." So there's plenty of distrust, but less fear than of religion or government.

Where does this put them on the continuum? Hard to say. On the one hand, the Great Recession of 2008 exposed some pretty hard feelings toward banks, investment brokers, and big business in general, crystallizing in the Occupy movement of 2011. On the other hand, we do not yet know where, if anywhere, the rush of populist sentiment will lead. The Tea Party movement and Occupy Wall Street seem to share many of the same concerns, but they also seem to be headed in very different directions. A lot of American do not trust big business or government or, for that matter, religions other than their own if they have one. But in a recent Gallup poll, when Americans were asked which concerned them more about the future of their country—big business, big government, or big labor—about two thirds said "big government" and fewer than 25 percent said "big business." We live in a society infused with distrust of institutions of all kinds, so maybe flea market dealers are just the least embedded among the unenthused.

The dealers distrust banks and insurance agents, but they don't distrust everyone. Indeed, they *do* trust most of the other dealers in the flea markets and choose to trade with other small, independent business people if they can. Flea market sellers profess to really like flea markets and to enjoy the camaraderie of other dealers. Outsiders are often (understandably) leery about the quality of the goods sold at markets where caveat emptor applies across the board. But the dealers are generally quite comfortable doing business with one another, not least because they are tied by past and future dealings, however tenuous, with those around them. As in any joint human endeavor, a certain sort of camaraderie applies and it is surely cheaper to conduct trade, whether sale or barter, off the books. So trust is not impossible, but it occurs face to face over long chunks of time in this community of very limited liability.

The dealers are committed to individual freedom, so they embrace capitalism as a principle because it is quintessentially American. After all, they work in the most basic, entrepreneurial, direct-to-consumer marketing situation imaginable. But when pressed about the corporate world, many express a populism that lays bare a crucial truth: their distrust of corporate cronyism trumps their commitment to the free-market ideal. They may like capitalism in principle, but they believe the system is stacked against them in the real world. On this, they may be at the edge of the spectrum, but a lot of people—including a lot of people reasonably termed redneck—are somewhere near them.

This undercurrent of populism defies the "red state," pro-Republican stereotype often hung on rednecks. The dealers are concerned that Mexican immigration is taking jobs and that NAFTA is giving smaller countries an unfair advantage and they blame Republicans. They know working people, often in lower-end hourly jobs, shop in flea markets. When those working people do not have cash in their pockets, they are not buying, so flea market vendors are unlikely to support the sort of free-market, trickle-down economics that begin by benefiting corporate capitalists. Not enough capitalists buy diabetic socks or knock-off DVDs at flea markets.

The dealers' economic populism was a little bit of surprise to me, but the populist anger during the Great Recession, which came after my research, helped me see it in context. I met many of the last people alive who admit voting for Ross Perot and who thought Jesse Ventura was great as governor of Minnesota. The dealers believe in capitalism in principle, but they are so certain the system is stacked against them that they are happy for politicians to champion the cause of "the little guy" or "the middle class." They are alienated from their own ideals, which can be a tough pill to swallow.

I had to stop and think carefully about what the dealers had to say. I am generally pro-market and pro-capitalism. It is not that I think markets and capitalism solve every problem, it's just that I trust the tyranny of money more than I trust the tyranny of political power. I honestly believe money is more available to everyone, in principle, than political power despite the best intentions of democracy. In the end, businesses are less directly coercive.

But the dealers have a point. Despite the fact they did not inherit money and did not get the benefits of first-class education, they are willing to take on the system as independent entrepreneurs. They are willing to slug it out in capitalism and to take care of themselves if that is the price of independence. But if the system is rigged against them and the rich are all in cahoots, with political and economic power locked up together, then the dealers don't see any chance for themselves.

I think Marx and his admirers would say that capitalism has sold the dealers a bill of goods. It has left them out there as isolated individuals believing that they could still succeed as economic individuals striving for the American dream. They should instead align themselves with the proletariat, the working class, but they have been so alienated and frustrated in the work environment that they splintered off into a million tiny fragments. It is difficult to organize labor within the business sphere—fewer Americans each year are members of unions—so organizing individuals like the dealers is nearly impossible.

Despite the fact that they might be better off as a part of an organized group and might be making things harder for themselves by staying aloof, I sympathize deeply with the dealers' desire to go it alone. Nobody tells them how to wear their hair or what time to start or stop each day. Their freedom may be illusory, from a macro-scale economic point of view, but it's pretty real in terms of the choices they get to make day to day. Their real opportunity is tightly circumscribed—more tightly than they can possibly imagine—but within that circle they can do as they damned please.

And here I sit, wearing a beard and an earring and writing about a project I took on as an independent craftsman. I belong to organizations and institutions, but I tend to hold them at arm's length (a luxury afforded by my wife's years in a high-paying job). I conducted these interviews and wrote this book entirely independent from the research centers and universities where I have worked at various times.

I see the problems the dealers face in staying outside the system and even understand, I believe, how staying independent might not always be in their overall best interest. Their kind of negative, individual freedom—*freedom from* coercion and authority—is weaker in some people's minds than the kind of *freedom to* that comes with political and economic security found usually in the unity of groups and in the insurance of social safety nets. But in a world where they do not trust groups—neither business nor government—to look out for their interests, I understand why they choose *freedom from*, why they'll take their chances just being left alone. I bet most readers who work for someone else understand it too.

4

Flea Market Jesus

"**M**Y BELIEFS WOULD PROBABLY scare the hell out of them," Cochise said as we started the interview about his religious views.

"What do you mean?"

"My beliefs don't fit into any particular denomination. I believe in reincarnation. I believe in things from Hinduism, Buddhism, and Christianity. If I went into a regular church, they wouldn't know what to do with me."

This wasn't the time to try to explain to him that many Christian churches are full of people who patch together different, eclectic beliefs into one more or less coherent worldview that works for them. So I pressed harder on church attendance.

"If you believe so strongly in God, then why don't you want to be part of a community that believes the same?"

"To be honest," he told me, "I just never have seen a reason to. I'm just not sure that what they're preaching is the true meaning of life. I've been in Catholic churches, I went to prayer in a mosque when I was in the army, I've been to holy rollers. Every one of them is sure that what they're saying and doing is true, but it just doesn't ring true to me."

"But don't you think the pews are filled with other people just like yourself, people who are searching for answers and who realize that nothing they get is going to be the whole story?"

"No, I guess I don't. I mean, I know there are other people in there with more questions than answers, sure, but there are an awful lot of people in there who already think they have all the answers. And a bunch of them are hypocrites. You know, I'll show up one Sunday and they'll say, 'Cochise, we've missed you. Where have you been?' And I want to say, 'Missed me? Dude, where were you when I was in the hospital with hepatitis? Where were you when I needed somebody to talk to?' Missed me, hell. They missed having me put my envelope in the plate."

"The envelope?"

"I mean the money. A lot of it is about building the new fellowship hall or being a big man in the church. People get all dressed up in their fancy clothes, then look down on people who aren't well dressed even while they're preaching about doing unto others as you would have them do unto you. I know a lady who went to the same church for years and years. She got real sick and couldn't go for three weeks in a row. Did anyone come visit her? No. Instead, her husband gets an envelope in the mail saying she is not up-to-date on her pledge. Now that's a bunch of crap."

"Do you really think they're all like that?"

"I just think there's some of that in all of them."

Cochise listens to other points of view, but they don't often change his mind. Now in his sixties, he's seen enough to figure out where he stands. I think back to all those years I had known him as a clingy drunk—gentle and friendly, even quiet and thoughtful, early in the day and aggressively more attached as the afternoon wore on and the beers wore him down. When someone said, "Alcoholics don't make friends, they take prisoners," they were talking about Cochise.

But the alcohol is gone now, leaving just a tired, aging man whose face shows every inch of wear. He still smoked non-stop until about two years ago—mostly tobacco, a little dope on the odd social occasion—and his voice is a raspy baritone punctuated with coughs. He's through the worst of the "Higher Power" addiction too. He'll still tell you about his spiritual journey out of the drunken abyss if you ask, but he's been on the wagon long enough to know that his friends have heard all the sermons before.

"Think about it," Cochise demanded. "Why do we need organized religion? It's a bond, a kind of social control. They want you to commit to this or that, to pledge this or that, to say that you agree with their definition of right and wrong. There's no freedom there. You know, whatever religion your parents were or your girlfriend is, that's the one you end up in. It's one more way to keep you in line."

"It's like Alcoholics Anonymous. I went until I got myself turned around, but AA is like church, it's just a boat to get to the other side.

Now, if you want to stay there once you arrive, that's ok. Maybe your story can help other people. But not everybody needs to stay. Once you become that kind of person, maybe you don't need the group in the same way."

"Like anything else, it's hard to just be around church, to just drop in and listen. They want you to get involved. They smother you, ask you to do stuff. I know sometimes they think they're doing you a favor by trying to include you, but it's just one more place where they take away your privacy and tell you what you should be doing instead."

"Did you go to church when you were young?"

"Yeah, my grandmother took me. She'd take me to Sunday school and then I'd meet her back in the main hall for the service. My parents didn't go, but they made sure I got up in time to be ready for grandma."

"And did something happen there that put you off."

"Not there specifically, no. I mean, the Sunday school teachers were nice enough ladies and they always brought cookies. I don't remember much of what the preacher said, but I'm sure it was the usual stuff."

"But I do remember other times that really put me off. Like the time a friend took me to Vacation Bible School in the summer and two adults got me off into a room by myself and started telling me how important it was that I accept Jesus into my heart. They kept asking me over and over whether I would pray along with them that Jesus would come into me and save me. Finally I agreed because I was too scared not to. I thought I might never get out of that room."

"The next summer, I convinced that same friend to skip Bible School and come swimming with me. One of those same teachers saw us. He came over and told us that if we thought swimming was more important than learning about Jesus, we were going to Hell. He said he wouldn't pray that we went to Hell, but he would pray that Jesus taught us the error of our ways. I was a year older and a little more stubborn by then. I didn't say anything, but I remember thinking 'fuck you, man.' So that was it for me and the born-again Christians. I didn't really spend any time with them again until some of my friends in AA had Jesus as their higher power."

"So what's your relationship to God like now?"

"I'm in the worldwide church of God, you know? I'm out here in the world, and this is God's church. And when I'm out in nature, like we are now, camping out here under stars, then I'm in the holiest place there is. How can you look at these trees and flowers and birds and think that the most important thing about God comes from sitting in a pew on Sunday morning?"

"Can you imagine ever going back to church? I mean, if you found the right pastor or the right group of people?"

"Sure. Anything's possible. But with everything in the news today, I don't think there are many pastors like that."

"Are you saying you don't trust clergy?"

"I'm saying I sure don't trust them any more than I trust anybody else. Look at all the priests with the young boys. Look at Jimmy Swaggart with the prostitute or Jim and Tammy Faye with the drugs and the money or that fellow [Ted Haggard] out in Colorado."

"But you don't think they're all like that, do you?"

"No. But they're all just regular human beings. They want to get ahead. They want to get money for that new church building. They want to move up to a better church."

"My relationship to Jesus doesn't come from preachers or from those other people in the church. It is personal, just between me and God. Why do I need to listen to them tell me what the Bible says when I can read it for myself?"

"So do you?"

"Do I what?"

"Do you read the Bible?

"I read it sometimes. I know a lot of the major stories. But I don't read it all the time."

"Do you believe it is God's Word?"

"I do. I believe God inspired the Bible. I mean, I don't believe it is word-for-word God speaking and someone is just sitting there writing it down—you know, except for maybe the Ten Commandments, when that really did happen—but I believe that God inspired the writers to know what to say."

"So do you believe the Bible should be taken as God's literal word, that it is absolutely infallible?"

"No, people wrote it down and people make mistakes. So there's no sense saying that every word of it is literally true. Some of the details are probably wrong, but I imagine they got the gist."

"Let me ask you this, then: do you believe Adam and Eve were real people who lived in a real garden?"

"I do. I mean, we had to start somewhere, right? God had to create somebody first. I'm not saying their names were really 'Adam' and 'Eve,' but God had to make someone first to get the whole thing started."

"So you definitely believe that God created the world as it is today."

"Well, not exactly as it is today. There used to be dinosaurs and now there's not. If you look on a map you can see that South America and Africa probably used to be hooked together, and now they're not. But I definitely believe God created the world. If you look around at it, you just see it is so complex and so perfect. You can't really think that the trees got there by accident, or that we just happen to have the four different seasons every year. And especially human beings: nothing as complicated as a human being just happened along. It had to come from somewhere. Someone or something had to do it."

"The stories that come after Adam and Eve, like Noah and the Ark, or Moses and the Ten Commandments, or Samson—do you believe those?"

"I do and I'll tell you why: when you get right down to it, why wouldn't I believe them? Any God who could create this world and create human beings to live in it and make everything work together so perfectly like the sun and the rain to grow the plants, why couldn't He tell Noah to build an ark or give Moses the laws or give Samson the strength to pull down the temple? I wasn't there, I didn't see it happen, but if I know there is a God who can make the world, why wouldn't I believe He could do those other things too? Why would those stories be in the Bible for all these thousands of years if God didn't want them in there? The Bible is the oldest book in the world. It's lasted it all this time for a reason."

"Do you ever have a problem believing any of it?"

"I'll tell you what I have a problem believing—when some preacher uses the Bible to say that Catholics can't marry Protestants or Christians can't marry Jews, or when people say that the races should be separate. Show me in there where it says that. That's what I have a problem with, when people try to tell you that the Bible says that you ought to be doing what they are preaching is right, but it's just their interpretation, it's not what the Bible says in plain fact. That's what I don't understand."

"You don't have any problems believing the miracles, then? You believe that Mary was a virgin, that Jesus turned water into wine, that he healed the lepers, or the big one, that he came back from the dead?

"I don't have any trouble believing any of those. I know God can work miracles. He's done it for me. And if He can reach into the world and do a miracle for Cochise, I think He can do pretty much anything he wants for his only Son. The problem isn't in believing that any of those happened, the problem is when people want to use those to get me to do what they want because they read the Bible, and they want me to read it, in just one certain way."

"What about *Revelation* and the rapture and the end of the world? Do you think Jesus is coming back any time soon?"

"I just don't know what to think about that one. *Revelation* is tough to read. People say they know what it's about, they know that something is a symbol of Israel or Iran or nuclear bombs or whatever. They'll say that this war or some other event is the same things being predicted in *Revelation* as part of the end times. That guy on television with the scary wife, what's his name . . ."

"Jack Van Impe and Rexella," I interject.

". . . Yeah, Jack Van Impe and Rexella. They're so sure that this or that event is the exact sign being talked about in the Bible. But how do they know that? Plus, haven't some people been saying the world was about to end for hundreds of years? I guess someone's bound to get it right one of these years, but I don't see why it's going to be tomorrow any more than 1000 years ago or 10,000 years from now. Different people have their signs of the end times, but that can only go on for so long before you say, 'you know, dude, maybe you don't have that exactly right.'"

As I listened to Cochise talk, I found myself wondering whether or not he was what people mean by *fundamentalist*. That term gets used a lot in America today to describe people who believe the Bible is literally true. Here was someone who explicitly said he did not believe that the Bible was inerrant word-for-word, but who clearly believed that all of the stories, even the creation myths, were actual historical accounts.

By historical reckoning, Cochise seems to believe many of the things fundamentalists are supposed to believe. The term "fundamentalist" was coined in the early 1900s in a series of scholarly essays aimed at defending the "fundamentals" of Christian faith against the threat of modern liberalizing. Those first fundamentalists insisted that the traditional, literal understanding of the virgin birth, miracles performed by Jesus, his bodily resurrection, and his eventual return in the Rapture was correct and that liberal attempts to interpret these as symbolic were dangerously misguided.

By that account, then, Cochise certainly seems like a fundamentalist. But when I hear him talk about reincarnation or his reluctance to join a church, I have to wonder: does he really belong in the same category as the late Jerry Falwell of the Moral Majority or James Dobson, longtime head of Focus on the Family? He's a literalist—he says he is. But is he a fundamentalist? And if he is, is he an "evangelical"?

The obvious answer is "no." Cochise is part of a *very* large segment of America that holds literal views of scripture, but by no means are all of those people part of the red state, evangelical, conservative resurgence offered as one side in the so-called culture wars. In America, belief in Biblical literalism is neither special nor odd. A third of Americans—100,000,000 people—believe the Bible should be understood literally. And another 47 percent believe it is the inspired word of God. This means that for about 80 percent of Americans—four out of every five—the Bible was provided directly by the Almighty Himself. Cochise is not exactly out on a limb.

But he *is* different from the literalists who believe that their reading of scripture leads to an obvious, unchangeable understanding of what God wants people to do. When those fundamentalists read the Bible literally, it tells them to attend church faithfully, give offerings to the church willingly, and raise a family according to a standard set of moral dictates. They read the Bible regularly, always within a predetermined theological frame of reference. They use scripture to create rules and guidelines. They try to make the stories of the Bible their stories, to live out their lives according to the narrative they see developing throughout the Bible. And make no mistake: they see the Bible as a straight-line, chronological story that begins in Genesis and ends in Revelation. The Bible is not a mystery; they know already how it comes out. And it is not merely non-fiction, it is a reference work.

Cochise, on the other hand, rarely reads the Bible at all. He believes the stories are true because they were told to him as true and because their explanation of events, especially the creation of humans, seems more plausible than his understanding of other potential explanations. He believes the miracle stories not because he is certain they are right, but because it is right to believe them.

In graduate school I learned the difference between "Big F" and "little f" fundamentalists. Some of the "little f" fundamentalists are the literalists like Cochise. They believe that most of the events described in Scripture actually happened in history. Most of the time they do not distinguish among stories; Adam and Eve in the garden, Moses with the Ten Commandments, or Jesus being raised bodily from the dead all carry the same valence. Each of these happened in "biblical times" and each teaches us something about our lives today.

For the "little f" fundamentalists, these stories do not require argument or defense. They are what "everyone" believes. A useful way to understand this is to think of a small town with only a couple of churches. People are surrounded by neighbors who believe much as they do. A straightforward, literal understanding of Scripture is taken for granted. People who disagree, or who have serious questions, either learn to keep their mouths shut or come to be thought of around town as eccentric.

Now imagine those "little f" fundamentalists moving to the city where they are confronted by a variety of beliefs and opinions. They are set cheek to jowl with Christians who hold symbolic or metaphorical views of some, or all, of the great biblical events. Beyond that, they are confronted by a wider population that does not read, or reads but does not believe, these stories at all. They meet people of other religions and of no religion.

In that situation, some literalists react defensively. They insist that their reading of the Bible is traditional, orthodox, and true, and they try various strategies to shape society based on that truth. These are the "Big F" fundamentalists, the ones who are very consciously promoting their understanding of the Bible as a challenge to the many faces of unbelief. Some mystified critics think the problem is that these Bible-believers fail to understand the importance of science and reason, that they somehow do not recognize what modernity is all about. But those critics are wrong. "Big F" fundamentalists *do* understand the importance of science and reason. They see all too clearly what modernity is about: putting individual understanding and interpretation at the center of the universe. The "Big F" fundamentalists are offering a conscious challenge and a clear Biblical alternative with God and God's Word at the center instead.

I did not know it at the time, but I was a "little f" fundamentalist as a child. I believed what everyone around me believed. In my first two years of high school, I began to experience my earliest challenges, or, perhaps more accurately, I began to understand that individualism and modernity and diversity *were* challenges to my literalist worldview. Interestingly, as I look back on it I realize that these challenges were introduced not by my peers but by my teachers. It's not as if I had suddenly been thrown in among atheists or followers of other world religions; kids at my high school were much like me. But my teachers consistently exposed me to a wide range of ideas and tried to draw me outside myself. This is what they are trained to do: to teach kids to think creatively by exposing them to new ideas. I now look back on their efforts with sincere gratitude, but it is any wonder that fundamentalist parents are so suspicious of public high school education and even more suspicious of non-religious college education? My teachers did for me exactly what fundamentalist parents fear teachers will do to their children: they taught me that critical, independent thinking was the foundation for knowledge and that *all* interpretation was *relative* to the historical context and the location of the person doing the observing. A few of them probably taught me that without even knowing they were doing it, but they taught me just the same. They gave me the stuff and I connected the dots.

At first, I reacted to those early challenges as I had been trained: I got even more religious, wearing the "I Found It" button and carrying my Bible. But in my case, it didn't last. The appeal of freedom and reason and individualism and scientific method were much too strong. From my old, literalist point of view, I made a conscious decision to put reason and logic at the center of my world. Put more bluntly, from a literalist perspective, I removed what I had been told about God from the center, replacing Him with my own ability—right or wrong—to experience, think, and understand.

Those changes had consequences. I went to a secular liberal arts college rather than a conservative Christian one. I switched from the traditional political conservatism of my parents to libertarianism. I abandoned my preoccupation with religion and revelation for a new interest in philosophy and analytical thinking. I got over that last one, at least the philosophy part, and came back to studying religion, but I had learned to approach it as a critic, later an ethicist, later a sociologist. Religion became the object, not the subject.

Cochise, like most of my flea market friends, is "little f" fundamentalist. He believes the Bible literally, just as I once did, because that is how it was told to him. I was trained to substitute science or reason or logic for traditional, revealed explanations; he was not trained like that. He has no cause to find Darwin's story of natural selection any more compelling than the Genesis stories his grandmother told him. His literalism is only thinly connected to the kind of political organizing and family values marketing done by "Big F" fundamentalists. Cochise is not defending his traditional beliefs against the onslaught of challenges from other religions or from secular science. Like the rest of us, he is using the tools he has to make sense of a complex world.

If you look in most Americans' real toolboxes, you're unlikely to find a matched set, laid out in order, with color-coded handles. Most of us have a mix of screwdrivers and wrenches from different manufacturers jumbled in together. We may have two box wrenches at the 5/8" size and none at 3/4." This is because some tools were handed down to us, some were bought at yard sales, and others were bought at the store because we needed one specific piece for a project.

Sociologist Ann Swidler has suggested that we each also have a cultural toolkit we use to make meaning out of the events in our lives. I hope I'm not damaging her portrayal by suggesting that most of us have cultural toolkits as mixed and rigged as our real toolboxes. Some people have a master plan, an overarching story, which they use to organize the whole range of things they think and believe. But these people are rare, and even their carefully organized toolboxes probably have more variation than they'd like to admit. Most of us aren't even close; we piece together many different strands as best we can and the overarching story is sketchy at best.

Many Americans, including many Christians, will understand Cochise's willingness to cobble together various philosophies and theologies into his own, eclectic, mix. This process of picking, choosing, and mixing enjoys a long history stretching well back into our colonial past. Even among the Puritans, some of world history's greatest sticklers for going by the Book, regular people believed in magic and astrology.

Even those Christians who understand the concept of creating one's own mix of beliefs and ideas might find it harder to swallow Cochise's unwillingness to say that a good, spiritual life depends on churchgoing. The majority of believers belong to a religious congregation. Here, Cochise's independence seems to be drawing on experiences very different from what mainstream Christians consider normal. Consciously or not, he is using tools that seem to push and pull in different directions.

Cochise doesn't belong to a congregation, but that's not the only thing that separates him from the evangelicals (only some of whom are fundamentalists) who are so visible in American public life today. He does not read the magazines like *Christianity Today*. He doesn't watch evangelical programming on television or listen to Christian radio. Those churchgoing evangelicals take part in many shared institutions that shape their understanding of the Bible and turn their belief into faith and their faith into action. Evangelicalism is what sociologists and anthropologists call a *subculture*, complete with its own toys, music, and media of all kinds. Cochise shares some of the beliefs, but they do not play out as faith or action because they are unattached to the other elements in that subculture. His ideas float freely, linking up to other folklore or political ideas or almost anything else. His beliefs are not channeled into a religious worldview. They do not become a way of life.

There are good reasons to believe that Cochise is not alone, no matter how much he wants to be a rugged individualist. A significant minority of Christian believers do not belong to congregations. The taken-for-granted linkage between literal belief and church membership is actually pretty weak.

The General Social Survey is one of the best measures of American ideas and practices covering a very wide range of topics. According to the survey in 2008, 76 percent of Americans say they believe in God, with another 10 percent saying they believe in a "higher power" but not a personal God. A figure around 85 percent for "believers" is essentially undisputed. Survey after survey finds that between 80 percent and 90 percent of Americans believe; the discrepancy comes both from sampling differences and from how the question is phrased, but nearly everyone grants that 85 percent is in the ballpark.

Despite this very high percentage of believers, fully 21 percent of Americans say they attend worship services "never," another 7 percent say they attend "less than once a year," and another 14 percent say they attend "once a year." That means about 40 percent of the population—approximately 120 million people—is unaffiliated with a congregation. Some of these who don't attend probably consider themselves loosely connected to their family's religious traditions. For instance, they probably have family congregations used for marriages and funerals, but they do not think of themselves as regular members or even participants.

We know that 40 to 50 percent of Americans consider themselves congregation members with another 10 to 15 percent who attend more than one or twice a year but are not members. On any given weekend, between 25 and 35 percent of Americans attend worship, depending on which study you are reading.

The exact numbers are not important for this discussion; year to year variation is relatively small. But it is very important to notice the very large gap between the 85 percent who say they believe in God and the 60 percent or so who attend worship more than once or twice a year. Something like one-fourth of all Americans fall into this category. This means there are 75 million pretty traditional believers out there who don't practice their beliefs by participating in congregational worship. Cochise is one of them.

At this point, some readers are screaming at the page in front of them, "but not all those believers are Christians. Maybe they believe in a different religion that does not revolve around a congregation. Maybe they have invented a religion of their own." No doubt some of them are doing just that. Some among that 75 million are involved in Eastern religions or New Age movements or some other form of spirituality, very possibly a mixture they have created for themselves. When the media portrays religious individualists, those are the kinds of people we see.

But it is clear that the large majority of those individualists—the believers who do not attend—hold plain, vanilla, even literalist, Christian beliefs. Sticking with the General Social Survey, 14 percent of those who say they *never* attend worship also say that the *Bible is the actual word of God and is to be taken literally*. This strongest case of people who do not attend and take the Bible literally includes 10 million people, a number larger than the membership of the United Methodist Church. Add in people who say they attend less than once per month and the number nearly triples. Add in those who take the weaker view that the Bible is the "inspired Word of God" and it grows even larger.

There are a lot of literalists out there who never, or rarely, attend worship. Most of those 75 million religious individualists are not devotees of some new philosophy or of "foreign" religions; most believe instead that the Bible is literally true or divinely inspired. They share some of the same theological understandings with organized fundamentalism, minus the institutions, the media, the doctrinal consistency, and the political opinions.

Fundamentalism—the "Big F", activist, kind—is a middle-class phenomenon. It is common among people faced with cosmopolitan diversity, but these are people who deal with that diversity by moving to relatively homogeneous suburbs. Although this way of thinking intentionally resists some aspects of modernity, it is itself thoroughly modern in other ways. It tends to make sense for people who appreciate an early twentieth-century view of science, often called "Baconian," in which direct experience and observation are the keys. It is *not* theoretical. That is why, for instance, supporters of creationism and Intelligent Design will argue that evolution is a flawed theory because we cannot actually *observe* it in action, we only infer it from millions and millions of pieces of fossil evidence. (They are wrong about this—we can see adaptation and natural selection directly in the mutation of bacteria—but that is beside the point here.)

The literalists, or "small f" fundamentalists, are usually poorer and less well-educated. Almost half of those whose family income is below $10,000 believe the Bible is God's actual, literal word, and the percentage of literalists goes steadily down as income goes up. About half of those with less than a high school education take the Bible literally, a percentage that goes down even more rapidly as education increases; only 10 percent of those with a graduate degree would say the same.

But here is what surprises many people: the poorest and least well educated Americans are not only the most literal about the Bible, they are also the *least likely* to attend worship. According to the 2002 General Social Survey, among those making less than $10,000 per year, fully *49 percent* attend less than twice a year, with *28 percent* never attending. Some older theories portrayed religion as a compensation, a philosophy used by the poor to convince themselves that their real reward would be in the hereafter. There may be some truth to this, but this hoped-for compensation does not lead to church attendance. Poverty relates positively to the belief that the Bible is literally true, but negatively to worship attendance.

As I promised at the outset, I have no intention of trying to explain away my flea market friends' literalism by reducing them or their ideas to social class or education or any other simplistic, deterministic interpretation. Instead, I want to consider what their combination of beliefs—about religion, about politics, and about business—says about American society. The question is not the condescending "what does this really say about them?" but "what does it say about all of us?"

I believe it says *they are not much different from the rest of us.* They say they have literal religious beliefs, including beliefs about the Bible, and that they model their lives on those beliefs and those stories, but they don't have any coherent theology and they don't even read the Bible. I say this is not unusual, but normal. It is more likely to work that way for most people than the all-encompassing picture of religion conjured by many who talk about it. The problem is not that the dealers are all over the map; the problem is that we—and I include religion researchers here—pretend that reality is more coherent and that we can predict what people will think or do by knowing enough of their story to pigeonhole them correctly. We can't, because inconsistency and mixed messages are the norm, not the exception.

People like Cochise do not fit the red-state stereotype. If I learned nothing else from my flea market interviews, I learned that. In one sense, this is not news; thoughtful people realize that most dichotomies are badly-drawn caricatures. Academics often make their living by drawing attention to the many shades of gray that lie between popular conceptions of issues as black or white. But this is not just about gray. In this case, the false dichotomy between educated progressives and uneducated traditionalists literally pulls our national conversation in the wrong direction.

Cochise is part of a large group of literalists who believe some very traditional things about the Bible but strongly resist a wide range of other traditional or conservative social conventions. Neither Cochise nor his flea market colleagues have bought into the whole happy story of middle class values embedded in middle class institutions. For instance, many dealers do not live in traditional nuclear families with husband, wife, and children. Everyone knows, of course, that many middle class Americans also live outside those kinds of families, but there is a difference: the middle class still holds that model up as an ideal, even if many fail to realize it in their own lives. For the dealers, family arrangements are a personal choice. They don't presuppose that there is only one way to live and so do not presuppose that the Bible offers unambiguous support for that way alone.

The same logic applies to church-going. Many middle-class Americans attend worship and participate in church social functions on a regular basis even if they lack strong ideological or emotional commitment. The flea market dealers might call them hypocrites, but I doubt if most of the "weak believer" church members would describe themselves that way. They are interested in knowing about God and living a good life and doing the right thing even if they are not strong believers. They see church as taken-for-granted, as a place where decent people meet to discuss their ethical obligations and to make sure that their children receive appropriate moral instruction. In many smaller towns, church membership is a badge of propriety, a visible sign that someone is morally upright, or at least that she tries to be.

The dealers work Sundays. Many are transient, at least during the warm season. When they have permanent homes, those homes are often out in the country where taxes are lower and where their comings and goings would not be public knowledge. But what really separates them from the middle class churchgoers is that they do not depend on relationships of mutual trust to manage ongoing business or personal dealings. An insurance salesperson or middle manager needs to be known in the community as someone who can be trusted; very often, she needs the informal connections of congregational membership just as she needs contacts in professional or fraternal groups. But the flea market dealer simply provides goods in exchange for cash, often to people he will never see again.

The middle class literalists who attend worship, and who are much more likely to be "Big F" fundamentalists, see the Bible as the rulebook that guides the orderly society they wish to live in. They live within a fairly all-encompassing framework and the Bible provides an essential part of the foundation. When these folks say that God forbids marriage between homosexuals or that women should be obedient to men in marriage, they are using sections from the rulebook that shore up their position. The truth of those propositions is guaranteed by the literal truth of other biblical claims such as the creation story or the bodily resurrection. The Bible validates their lives *and* it validates itself by being totally, consistently, literally true. If you give up on even one part of its literal truth, the whole social structure gets a little shakier.

Some of those beliefs make their way to people like Cochise, but as odds and ends of cultural knowledge, not as a fixed, coherent system of rules and obligations. It's okay with him, because he's not nearly as worried about that middle class social structure.

Most of the flea market vendors believe in creationism and in the bodily resurrection; some, though fewer than outsiders might suppose, agree that the Bible says gays should not marry or that women should be obedient. But they are not committed to these ideas the way "Big F" fundamentalists are, because for the "Big F" fundamentalists, nothing but a self-assumed model of rigid consistency will do. Critics may point out that there are other places where the "Big F" fundamentalists do not maintain that consistency, but those criticisms miss the point. The philosophy need not be consistent from an external perspective, it need only cohere internally in the minds of those who believe it.

Folk religion has many literalist elements, but it is not what most people mean by fundamentalism. It does not insist on philosophical consistency, does not make strong demands on believers, and does not lead to political or social imperatives. Believers in folk literalism may oppose gay marriage, but they may not. They may believe abortion should be stopped through social coercion, but they may believe individuals should be free to decide. They may believe kids should pray in school like they did in the good old days, but they may think it is better for each to believe as she chooses.

The folk believers share some of the tools in the "Big F" fundamentalist's toolkit, but they have many different—unmatched—tools in there too. And they see no problem with this, because their reading of scripture does not demand a rigid consistency with tight links to other philosophical beliefs about church membership, American patriotism, or the economy.

The folk believers, the "little f" fundamentalists, draw from many other traditions, including strong American strains of individualism and populism. As we have seen, their ideas about business cover a wide spectrum. Their ideas about politics do too.

Understanding the distinction between folk believers and what most people mean by fundamentalists, or evangelicals for that matter, is crucial. We will never really appreciate the flea market dealers for who they are unless we understand that their biblical beliefs mix easily with many other kinds of beliefs. Their literalism does not lead them to an analytical consistency that sweeps all other ideas and experiences from its path. Unless we disabuse ourselves of the notion that believing in

Adam and Eve as real people automatically leads to a fixed set of conservative social beliefs, we cannot truly hear Cochise or his colleagues speaking for themselves.

You might ask yourself, "If this folk religion does not lead to a consistent philosophy and lifestyle, is it religion at all? Do these people really believe anything, or do they just feel like they should say they do?"

It's a reasonable question. Americans frequently tell pollsters and interviewers what they want to hear. Or maybe more to the point, they tell them they do the kinds of things they think they should do, the things they imagine themselves doing somewhat regularly. A much higher percentage of folks say they attend worship "weekly" than are actually present on any given weekend. A much higher percentage of people say they always vote in elections than ever turn up for any particular poll.

But in this case, I am entirely convinced that the folk believers really believe, by which I mean they both think and feel these ideas to be true. Indeed, I'd guess that they have, as a whole, a much stronger sense of the supernatural, of God's intervention in everyday affairs, than even most "Big F" fundamentalists. Moreover, I'm also convinced that many of the people in so-called mainstream or traditional religion have toolkits that are much more varied than they themselves imagine. If we set the threshold for calling something "religion" too high, we'll have to leave out a lot more people than just the dealers.

Out of 60 interviews, two people told me they did not believe in God. But the overwhelming number of people who call themselves believers is not the strongest evidence. The real proof is the number of people who recounted specific, detailed stories of miracles performed on their behalf. There were many tales of recovery from serious illness or surprising good luck in automobile accidents, but beyond those were incidents that made the hair on the back of my neck stand up.

One older gentleman described how depressed he was after his wife's death. He was visited in a dream by a white-haired, white-bearded stranger in white robes who led him to a mansion where he was comforted by his wife. When he awoke, his depression was gone and he began the process of recovering. But there's more. Turns out that same white-clad stranger had appeared to him twice before, once when he was a young soldier in Korea on the verge of nervous breakdown and once just before his first son was born. The angel even told him what to name the child—and he took that advice. After both visions he was calmed and restored.

Another fellow had a story about being miraculously saved from crushing in a crane accident. Cochise remembers when his friend's departed spirit visited him in the form of an eagle, and spoke to him, while he was fishing.

I have known all three of these men for more than twenty years. It is certainly possible that they were deluded or confused or mistaken, but there is no chance they were pulling my leg. They were describing what they interpreted as acts of divine intervention on their behalf.

People I just met told me other stories. Most revealing is the tale of a young woman who was praying for guidance. She had some balloons in her van and asked, "God, if this is what you want me to do, then please just pop one of these balloons so I'll know it's your will." No balloons popped. She walked over to a Pepsi machine and put in her two quarters. Just as she pushed the Pepsi button, she thought to herself, "No, I'd rather have Mountain Dew." A Mountain Dew rolled out the bottom. "So I said right there, well, sir, I don't need to ask you for nothing else," she recounted, "this is all the sign I need."

Another told me the story of being out of money—not an uncommon occurrence. While he was loading his car in the parking lot, a stranger walked up and offered him $150 for some fishing lures the dealer considered worthless. He regarded this stranger as an angel. And it's not the only angel story I heard. Another dealer talked about driving to the state fairgrounds when his car broke down. Out of nowhere, a stranger appeared and offered to fix it. The stranger then asked for a ride to the convenience store and gas station down the street. When the dealer went in to pay for gas, the stranger mysteriously vanished without ever asking for anything.

As you read this, if you don't recognize these stories as miraculous and as part of God's intervention on behalf of his children, then you do not inhabit the same mystical universe as many of the dealers. And if you're tempted to think that they are very odd cases way out on the cultural fringe, walk into any religious bookstore and ask to see the shelves with books on angels and divine guidance.

I do not experience the world as mystical or magical. But as long as I believe people are telling me the truth as they understand it, I don't make judgments about the validity of their claims. Whatever *really* happened with the white-robed angel, the eagle, the Pepsi machine, or the angelic mechanic, my respondents experienced these as instances where God was willing and able to act in their lives. Whether or not this constitutes "faith" depends on your theology, but it undoubtedly constitutes "belief."

And this is not some generic belief in a vague concept of God. My flea market subjects believe in God of the Bible, the God of Abraham whom Jesus called Father. In fact, as we have now seen, the large majority of them believe the Bible word for word.

But for the last time I emphasize that this group is not really a subset of the conservative evangelicals we hear so much about. They do not like the term "born again" and do not apply it to themselves. They do not usually watch television preachers or listen to religious programming on the radio. They don't read religious magazines.

This is why all of us must be very careful about lumping all "conservative" Christians into any large pot. Are these literalists "conservative" Christians? Well, they believe the Bible is literally true and they believe God is real and active in the world today. But this plays out in their lives very differently than it does for middle class, small town folk or upper middle class suburban-dwellers. This is literal religion but it's hard to say how it is conservative in any sense other than that it denies decades of modern intellectual development.

Keep this distinction in mind as we turn to politics, because the mix of religion and politics makes the distinction between these literal, folk believers and contemporary conservative evangelicals even clearer.

5

Cochise, the Dealers, and Politics

"THE LYING SONOFABITCH KNEW there weren't any weapons of mass destruction before we ever went in there."

"Come on, Cochise," I said. "All the available intelligence, from a lot of different countries plus the U.N., said the same thing."

"No they didn't. Those other countries' leaders knew better. They knew the U.S. would get rid of Saddam Hussein and so they let us do it. A few of them raised a fuss to keep their left wingers down, but they knew. Bush knew. Powell knew. The world just wanted a way to get rid of a dictator for free and Bush wanted a way to tell everyone they needed to re-elect him because of the war."

Clearly, I was interviewing in the midst of the Iraq invasion and occupation in the mid-2000s. But it wouldn't matter. I've had plenty of conversations since, and the feelings are the same—only the issues have changed.

"I don't trust any of them," Cochise went on. "Every one of them gets in a position where they need to lie to get something they want. Then once they start lying, it's hard to stop."

"Then why don't you vote against them, get them out of there?" I ask.

"Because you and I both know it doesn't matter. The one who spends most money buying the most ads is going to win. Neither candidate (in any election) gives a fuck what I think—and don't give me any of that bullshit about libertarians or socialists, because *nobody* gives a fuck what they think." Cochise knows about my libertarian streak and wanted to make sure I didn't slip a quick sales pitch in on him.

"But it could be different, right?" I asked. "I mean, the government could have the right kind of people in it if people would just vote in the right candidates?"

"I don't think so. It's too far gone. The way the government is set up now, you've got to be on the lobbyists' payroll to stand a chance in the election. And even if you were honest before the election, once you get in, you spend all your time trying to get re-elected. You start taking even more money from special interests. And that's when the lying starts and never stops."

Cochise had thought this through further than most dealers. I see plenty of bumper stickers that say "I love my country but fear my government" and I've heard that sentiment expressed a dozen different ways. But the conversations were often trite, tired rehearsals of catch phrases from people who were up against it. One lady about five booths down from Cochise put it most colorfully: "My government is a back-stabbing bitch, she will look at you and kill you and she will kill her own that is working for her." But Cochise wasn't just angry and confused; he perceived a story line, a coherent narrative explanation of why things are like they are. He saw a link between power and money that struck him as airtight.

I asked Cochise, as I asked everyone, whether he considered himself Democrat or Republican.

"Neither one," he replied. "They're just the same."

"What do you mean 'just the same'? "How can you say that? There are huge differences in their platforms and in their candidates."

"Maybe so, but none that matter to me. I'm not on either of their sides because, near as I can tell, neither of them is on my side."

In this, he is not alone. Only one in three of my interview subjects align themselves with a political party. They just do not see the affiliation as a significant part of who they are.

"So you're saying that it doesn't matter who's in office?"

"No. It matters somehow, I guess. But it just doesn't matter *enough to me*. I've got things to do. I've got places I want to go. There's no one saying anything enough different from what everyone else is saying to matter to me. Because in the end, neither side really wants to change the system."

"What system is that?"

"The one where the people with money pay off the people in government so they both get what they want."

"Are you saying you don't trust anyone in the government?"

"That's about it. I don't trust a one of them any more than I would trust any other stranger. I think that once people are put in a position of a certain amount of power, then there are opportunities that would be stupid for them to pass up. They have to abuse their power to take those opportunities, but I feel like any sane person who is put in that position is going to make mistakes, and I really think those mistakes are made a lot more often than anybody knows."

"Is there any way to fix the system?"

"Don't know. But ask yourself this: who would fix it? Who has enough power and money to get heard over the money and bullshit of the people who already have the power? People like Jesse Ventura or Ross Perot get a little attention for a little while, but in the end, who really cares what they think? Even with all of Perot's money, who really cared? Nobody. And you know why? Because everybody thought it was funny when Jesse Ventura stuck his finger in the big guys' eyes, but everybody really knows, deep down inside, that it doesn't change shit."

"Do you think that's why more people don't vote?"

"I know that's why. It's just not worth it. The politicians get some people all jazzed up over some meaningless crap like sex on television or gay marriage—something they can complain about but are never going to change. Then the jazzed-up people send in their money, to the politicians and to the television preachers. And those people vote to get sex off TV or to stop gay marriage. At the same time, the people who know it doesn't matter don't send in their money and they don't vote either. They figure their time is better spent either having fun or just trying to get by. At least that way they get something out of it."

Cochise's eyes flashed a hint of the angry alienation he was expressing, but the rest of his face betrayed his tired resignation. The rules were made by somebody else and, worst of all, there was no realistic way to fight back. Like so many Americans, and like virtually all the flea market dealers, he did the only thing he knew how to do: he withdrew. He pulled back into his shell and tried to wall his life off, far as he could, from a government he did not trust to look after his interests and which he feared did not trust him to look after his own.

The financial crisis of 2007 and 2008 just made this alienation worse. Most of the flea market dealers do not own expensive homes that lost value or mortgages that turned upside down. To them, this was a case of big-money special interests making huge profits on risky bets, then getting bailed out by taxpayer money when some of the bets went wrong. That "alienated" point of view got much broader around 2007 and 2008. And while some Americans took heart and hope in the Obama election of 2008, my flea market friends were not usually among them.

"The least they could do is just let me pay my taxes and then leave me alone."

"What do you mean?"

"Look, I've given up on hoping that the President or the Congress is going to make my life any better. I've given up hoping that they going to take less money out of my check, or make my life better with what they do take. But for Christ's sake they could at least just take the money and stay out of my business."

"Such as?"

"Gun control. Goddamned city boy politicians who have probably never been hunting and couldn't hit the side of a barn with a laser scope want to take away my guns to make the world safer. To make the world safer? I didn't drop any fucking bombs on Vietnam or Afghanistan or Iraq. I didn't put anybody in a secret prison down in Cuba. I never robbed a bank or shot anybody. I never asked for a bailout when my big plans went bad. But taking my guns is going to make world safer?"

"But President Bush didn't want to take your guns. He was one of the good guys, right?"

"On that, yeah, maybe. But only because he's always looking for ways to make enough people happy so his party gets 51 percent of the vote. If he can do that, then he can do what he really wants, which is to pay some big, fat contracts to his buddies in the oil business."

"So John Kerry would have been better?"

"In some ways, sure. More people work when Democrats are in. But it's Kerry and his big-city, Harvard, buddies who would take the guns. So I'm pretty much screwed either way."

"Is Harvard the problem with guys like Kerry?"

"Hell, no. Bush went to Harvard and to Yale. Did you know that both he and Kerry were in the same secret fraternity, Skull and Bones, at Yale? Big surprise. A bunch of rich kids learning the passwords and secret handshakes so they can help each other keep all the money."

"But it can't be just about money. I mean, there's the war. And abortion. And a bunch of other issues people really care about."

"You mean a bunch of issues that they tell people are important. Nobody likes abortion, nobody wants to kill babies. And I know some people feel so strongly about it that they'd give everything to stop it. But I'll tell you this about a lot of those fancy preachers and those women in nice clothes out there protesting abortion: if their 14-year-old daughter got pregnant, that's what they'd do."

"Fact is," he went on, "it's nobody else's goddamned business. Republicans go on and on about it, but they don't change it. And even if they get their guys on the Supreme Court, hell, even if they really change the law, people are still going to do it. Can't stop them."

"What about Iraq? Or Afghanistan? Or wherever we go next?"

"It's still all about getting in power and staying in power. With Vietnam, Johnson had to show that Democrats would stand up to communism. In Iraq, Bush needed to give people a reason to support him, to think that he was some big patriot protecting America from the bad guys. People were scared of communism then and they're scared of terrorism now. Only question is, which politician can convince them that he's the guy who'll keep them safe?"

"So it's about fear?"

"Fear and money. In Bush's case, it worked out perfect. The people who paid for his election make money selling weapons and they make money when the price of gas goes up. The people who don't have any money believe he's Captain America, a super patriot saving us from the bad guys. Perfect."

"But what about the morality stuff: rap lyrics? Sex on TV? Some people really care about those things, don't they? The parties really were different on those?"

"All bullshit. Do you watch TV? Then you know there's been more sex and more swearing every year for the past 30 years. And rock music and rap music are about sex and drugs and gangs and shooting, it never changes. And we've had Tipper Gore complaining about it and Jerry Falwell complaining about it and a thousand preachers pounding their Bibles and preaching hellfire. And what happens? Nothing. And you know why? Because the people who make the TV shows and sell the CDs are still getting paid."

"But can't people change the system if they get educated and vote?"

"Won't happen."

"Won't?"

"Nope. Not enough people care, and those who do care have already swallowed somebody's version of the story. They've stopped thinking for themselves."

"So all that's left is a revolution?"

"Nah. Nobody cares enough for that. Everybody's got color TV and plenty of quarter-pounders with cheese. Everybody knows somebody who doesn't have insurance, but most people still have it themselves, so they don't do anything. And the rich people are too smart to let a bunch of people die on the sidewalk because they don't have insurance. If that happened too often, maybe there really would be a fight. So they'll just bring in more Mexicans and let them go without insurance, because they can't vote anyhow and the rest of us don't notice if they get sick and can't see a doctor. The rich people will make sure it never gets too bad, not bad enough to start people thinking."

Looking back, I have to think Cochise's cynicism about revolution does not bode well for the present-day Tea Party. Or maybe even for Occupy Wall Street. He hit a vein of alienation, but could not see it heading anywhere. At the time, I wondered to myself where it might be headed, and the contours are not markedly clearer now.

Cochise was never part of the evangelical wing of the Republican Party that has been re-animated in the Tea Party and he has little hope of such a movement fundamentally changing American politics. The odds the Tea Party movement could sweep the populists like Cochise into the fray are long indeed. Could Occupy Wall Street? Surely not in its present form with students, young people, and anti-globalization activists.

Cochise looks at the ground, sighing and exhaling at the same time. I'd heard this story dozens of times during my interviews, sometimes told with anger, sometimes with stone-faced resignation. That the big guys work together to keep the little guys down is a truism in flea market circles. They tell me multiple versions, but the punch line is the same. And although I am trusted as an acquaintance by many of the dealers, I'm a close friend of very few. If this is what they say to me on tape, what must they say to their close friends in private after a few beers?

I saw both anger and resignation in Cochise, but mostly I saw disappointment. There was a palpable sense that something good had soured, that something precious had been lost. They see it in the Bush presidency and in Iraq and the financial crisis. They see it in the Obama presidency because of a vague sense that bigger government will mean more control of their lives, not less. I see this sense of loss all the time at Friendship, and not just among the flea market dealers. Even the shooters—the working class or middle class elite in the Friendship crowd— have a sense that the world is changing around them for the worse.

I conducted my interviews in the mid-2000s, but the mistrust of government, the disgust with Congress and, to a lesser degree, with the President, is greater, not less, as I finish this book in 2012. Whatever "hope bounce" the country got from the Obama election could not overcome the malaise caused by the economic disaster of 2007–08. "Bailouts" are the new watchword for how big government and big business have screwed the little guy again.

Neither the shooters nor the dealers are merely paranoid. The world of black powder shooters dealers really *is* deteriorating. The antiques really are gone from the flea markets, not counting the occasional real find in a box of junk. Black powder shooting has lost much of its appeal for a younger audience. Over the past twenty years or so, NMLRA membership has dropped from around 22,000 to about 16,000. But that's just the surface change. Many of the shooters are also Freemasons, an organization that has seen its numbers drop from 6 million to 1.5 million in the last half-century, pacing the changes described by Robert Putnam in *Bowling Alone*. A white, rural, working-to-middle class life characterized by hunting and fishing really has crumbled as labor jobs moved overseas and working Americans moved in from the farms toward the cities and suburbs. The shooters, especially the re-enactors in Primitive, are resisting in their own way—by clinging to a re-created past—just as the flea market dealers resist by refusing to have their lives determined by mainstream institutions. But they can see the writing on the wall.

Since I had Cochise opened up on the subject of bought politicians, I pressed on, hoping to see if this well had a bottom. To get my bearings, I started with the one question to which I always already knew the answer: "What is your opinion of how social welfare programs are handled in America?"

"The problem," said Cochise, "is that those who really need it don't get it, and those who get it don't need it." Of all the beliefs and ideas I heard during my interviews, this is by far the most widely held. Everyone has heard the stories of welfare fraud and most people personally know some able-bodied person who is getting assistance but should be out looking for a job. This is unshakeable working-class lore, best summed up in the bumper stickers that say, "Keep Working: Millions on Welfare Need the Money" or "If You Can't Feed 'Em, Don't Breed 'Em." But at the same time, most people know someone who is in a genuine jam, through no apparent fault of their own, and is having trouble getting help. To the dealers, the government appears to be strict and unreasonable about some claims while giving money to others who are less deserving. This is not bootstrap conservatism, not even the "teach a man to fish" philosophy. The dealers believe government should help people, they just feel like those people are not them—despite the fact many of them are on disability.

It's difficult to pin down the roots of this particular distrust. Some of it may be racial. There is a sense that minorities, once African-Americans, now also Mexican immigrants, get special treatment. There is a hazy assumption that when black people make a claim for assistance, bureaucrats at the imagined "welfare office" are sympathetic. But when poor whites describe similar circumstances, they are treated with suspicion. There is an undercurrent of belief that illegal immigrants still get special standing with benefits unavailable to working white people.

I have seen this concern about bias in poor whites before while studying religion in the neighborhoods of Indianapolis. Residents of the city's poorest "white" area, referred to by suburbanites as "Little Kentucky," complained that the mayor's "Building Better Neighborhoods" program never quite seemed to make it to their neighborhood. In their view, poor blacks were told that they needed social programs to level the playing field, but poor whites were told to get off their butts and get a job.

Once this talk was all about black people, but in Indiana, as in much of the U.S., you cannot spend much time in flea markets or gun shows without hearing someone mention all the Mexicans moving to the area. Mexicans are taking jobs because they are willing to work cheaply, some will say. The government doesn't enforce the laws for Mexicans the way it does for the rest of us, say others. But the most common and angry complaint is the classic: Mexicans do not have to pay taxes.

Part of popular lore is that recent immigrants of all kinds can avoid paying federal income tax so long as they do not become citizens. I know this because my father-in-law is a Scottish citizen who has lived in the U.S. as a resident alien for fifty years. To this day he can stir up a working class barroom by announcing that he sees no reason to get his citizenship papers, since then he would have to pay taxes. (Of course, he is, and always has been, required to pay taxes.)

The tax complaint is not entirely groundless. I'm sure some recent arrivals from Mexico manage to get paid cash under the table and avoid tax payments, though I feel safe in also assuming that they are working for wages far below normal scale. But for many immigrants, the problem is just the opposite: they get fake Social Security numbers so they can get jobs, have payroll taxes withheld on that fake number, and then never receive any of the benefits which their withholding helps underwrite.

From a logical point of view, a government policy of allowing immigrants to work without paying taxes makes no sense and is certainly not the law. My father-in-law, a resident alien, must pay taxes without getting to vote. The point is obvious: it would not benefit the government to allow people to get services without paying. But to the flea market dealers, as to millions of other people living below the middle class line, it makes perfect sense: rich business owners and government bureaucrats are in cahoots. It's not that they have any special affection for Mexican immigrants, but business needs a constant supply of cheap labor, government is willing to do what business pays it to do, and Mexicans are cashing in. Once again, everybody gets rich except the white working guy just trying to make a living. Once again, poor, average, people trying to do their best get screwed.

This worldview is very different from the kind of middle-class conservatism that sees America as the world's champion of democracy and land of free-market opportunity. Middle class conservatives favor capitalism because they believe they have a chance to get rich, or at least that the system is fair and rewards hard work and intelligence. But the flea market vendors, who are often culturally conservative about some traditional moral issues, see the ideal of America—opportunity and freedom—as something very different from the reality. They embrace the ideal, they just don't trust others to practice it.

This is another reason why the flea market dealers I spoke to are not today's Tea Partiers—even the most revolutionary Tea Party members tend to come from the middle class. They have a significant stake in the economic system, they just want a different balance between the economy and government, one that puts more emphasis on individual achievement and less on government redistribution for fairness.

But that is not the dealers' issue. They're not worried about more government per se, but about a link between elites in business and government. They are populists, not small-government conservatives, and there are more redneck populists like them than current analysis acknowledges.

The distinction dealers draw between the capitalist ideal and daily life can hardly be overdrawn. The flea market dealers are for God, Country, and the Free Market in principle. Those ideals are embedded in the myths and stories they've heard their whole life.

About half of the people I spoke with said they voted in the last presidential election (which at the time was Bush vs. Kerry, 2004). Whether or not they really voted, I cannot say. But, as I mentioned earlier, there is a powerful American ideology equating voting with good citizenship; the percentage of the general population who say they vote is much larger than the percentage who actually do. This corresponds to other similar data about "good" participation. People like to say they behave in ways they consider noble and think others will consider upright. The received wisdom is that Good Americans vote, so at least some of my respondents feel the pressure to perform their civic duty and some others feel at least enough pressure to *say* they do.

On the other hand, the half who tell me explicitly they do *not* vote can be harsh and firm about the reasons why not: they believe it does not matter. ("My government is a backstabbing bitch . . .") And whether they vote or not, they are clear about their distrust of the government whose future leaders are on the ballot. Four out of five respondents say they unequivocally do not trust the federal government, and state and local government fare little better.

Only a third of my respondents align themselves with a political party, with about equal shares Republican or Democrat. The other two-thirds think of themselves as independent. Despite the efforts of Ross Perot's Reform Party, Greens, libertarians, and socialists to energize the disengaged, not one respondent has claimed to belong to a third party, though a few mentioned Perot's distant candidacy favorably. These folks do not even like the more general labels: about one-sixth have said they were "conservative" and another sixth have said they were "liberal," but, again, two-thirds refused to place themselves even on that abstract spectrum. *They are not on anybody's side because no one is on their side.*

The dealers harbor deep suspicions about government but this does not mean they are ambivalent about America. The bumper stickers are right: even if they fear their government, they really do love their country because to them, it represents *freedom*. Said one, "We will all fight until we die to stay free because we don't know nothing but freedom. I mean you got freedom to come here and talk to me. I could've said 'no' or I could've said 'yes,' and if I had you would've gone on right to somebody else. You have got that freedom. Hey, man, we like freedom. I will fight until I die for freedom."

They really do embrace the *ideal* of America, but distrust the government, the institution that would seem to most clearly embody it. In government as in every other structure in their lives, these common folks see the elite bending the ideal to their own interests. They believe the stories, they just do not trust powerful strangers to live them out. They really do love their country, but they really do fear their government too.

This distinction might mean many things, including the possibility that the dealers are just chewing sour grapes. They believe in the ideals but have not done so well themselves, so it must be someone else's fault. But more than personal motivation or ability is at stake here. The disjuncture between *believing* the ideals and putting them into practice is jarring to the rest of us precisely because a link is missing. I believe that missing link has to do with the institutions most of us take for granted but some of us avoid. When there are no organizations, no symbols, no common language for putting ideals into practice, we are left with a palpable gap. I think the dealers' distrust comes from standing in that gap too long and too deeply.

I realized early on that if my interpretation is right, then there is a big difference between the "redneck" flea market dealers and the diehard Republican, working class, NASCAR dads most people think of when they think "Red State" politics. This distinction hit me as I worked on the article for *Christianity Today* magazine mentioned before: the biblical literalism of the flea market vendors is not the same as the biblical conservatism of the nation's evangelicals. The difference has everything to do with institutions, with the way beliefs are translated into daily activity.

The dealers hold many culturally conservative values, but they are not nearly as invested in moral conservatism as a dominant, consistent worldview. A politically conservative character is forged through involvement with school communities, political parties, non-profit groups, religious congregations, and mainstream media. The dealers opt instead for an individualism that protects and respects the distance they have created between themselves and such institutional control. Their specific political views, therefore, float in a gray area bordered by an individualism close to libertarianism, a cultural conservatism close to right-wing Republicans, and an economic populism closer to left-wing Democrats.

The tense issues of abortion and interracial marriage make the point nicely. Most dealers, like most Americans, dislike the idea of abortion. They wish women would not need to have abortions. But most of the dealers are also unwilling to outlaw abortion, unwilling to criminalize individual choice in the matter. Same goes for interracial marriage. Most, though by no means all, of the dealers think people should marry within their own race. But, again, they take a live and let live attitude when it comes to actual policy. They may have culturally conservative personal views but, unlike conservative evangelical Christians, they are unwilling to turn those into public policy.

Gun control, another controversial issue, makes the same point. Here, a culturally conservative attitude dovetails nicely with a laissez-faire stance on policy and the flea market dealers are much more certain of their position: hands off guns. There is no disjuncture here, no gulf between traditional values and individual choice. In gun control those sides meet and the dealers' opinions were nearly unanimous. The old bumper sticker line, re-invigorated by former NRA President Charlton Heston, comes easily from the mouths of flea market dealers: "They'll get my guns when they pry them from my cold, dead fingers."

Through the Lens of Distrust

Most people reading this book will have a tough time imagining life in a world where the system is always stacked against them, although this concern was highlighted to a much wider audience by the financial crisis of the late 2000s. The underlying belief that the rich and powerful control both business and government becomes a lens through which the world is viewed—it cannot help but color every other opinion. The concern has spread throughout America, but the sense of true alienation experienced by the flea market dealers surely has not.

I've heard colleagues suggest that the flea market dealers' attitudes about race, sexual orientation, and immigration are grounded in ignorance and fear. Maybe. But overwhelmingly the dealers themselves tell me they like other people, of whatever kind, as individuals, they just believe changes that work against them are being crammed down their throats.

Immigration is the easiest place to see this. As I mentioned before, the dealers rarely say anything bad about Mexicans as fellow human beings. The occasional whisper of "big drinkers" or "bad drivers" is more than offset by the number of times Mexicans are referred to as "hard working" and "friendly." Plain and simple: most of these white rednecks don't dislike Mexicans personally, though sometimes they fear large-scale cultural changes.

So what's the problem? They believe undocumented immigrants are taking money out of their pockets. Some economists will immediately counter that the undocumented immigrants are usually doing jobs that Americans do not want to do for a wage Americans would not accept. Moreover, companies would simply ship the jobs overseas if they could not find workers here.

Both things may be true, but they do not change the fact that the availability of undocumented labor, in the country illegally, affects wages. Someone must do tear-out work on a construction site. Someone must cut grass and pick up garbage. Someone must change hotel sheets, bus tables, and wash the dishes. If corporations, small businesses, and rich homeowners could not find undocumented immigrants to do this work for minimum wage or less, they would be forced to pay more to get it done. It is true that some of this comes back out of everyone's pocket in the form of higher prices, but it is also true that some of it comes out of the profits that wind their way to the top.

The effects do not stay on the bottom, either. If the grunt work can be bought for $8 an hour, then slightly more skilled, trusted work can be had for $10 an hour, so even the preferred class of laborers must take less for their effort. Put another way, if companies had to pay $10.00

to get enough workers to flip burgers and rake leaves, then they'd have to pay $12 or $14 to those who could assume more responsibility. Undocumented immigrants, especially non-English speakers, have to take what they can get. They set the floor on which all other labor wages stand.

For the most part, outsourcing works the same way for even higher end jobs. If computer programming can be done in India for $10 per hour, how many companies will continue to pay $50 per hour to U.S. workers? A new floor readjusts the expectations at every level. Who is more prejudiced? Is it Cochise, who sees clearly how a lax immigration policy pushes down labor wages, or those who blame his antipathy toward undocumented immigrants on his supposed fear and racism?

This is not a book about economic policy. There are real benefits in the economic growth fueled by a steady stream of cheap labor performed by immigrants, with some of those benefits accruing to the immigrant laborers themselves. But whatever side of that argument you might take, it doesn't make sense to blame the white working class for noticing they have been adversely affected by a government that does not enforce its own laws regarding immigration and citizenship.

The question of racism, especially toward Americans of African descent, is considerably trickier. Although I sensed little personal hostility toward Mexicans, a number of people took a negative view of what they saw as "black" culture. And, again, this is what people would say to me, a researcher holding a microphone. Who knows what they say in private?

Some of the dealers are racist. In every interview, I would ask "Of all the things that separate people and make it difficult for us to communicate and get along with one another, which one factor is most important?" Then I'd suggest, "It could be religion, race, ethnicity, money, the difference between men and women, or something else you'd care to suggest." No single answer stood out as dominant—in fact, the answer given more than any other had to do with character or upbringing because the dealers as a group value individual choices. But race was mentioned enough times to be worthy of consideration.

Like the majority of dealers, Cochise does not emphasize race. But some did. When I asked about the most important economic issue facing the world today, one dealer said "population." When I pushed a little, he said the real problem was that "unproductive" ethnic groups were the ones propagating the fastest. It's worth mentioning, though, that the same respondent said the idea of interracial marriage did not really bother him because "to each his own."

Most of the dealers agree. A few offered that people should marry among their own race—"on a farm, you don't mix chickens with goats"— but most tempered their opinions with the usual "I can't tell somebody else what to do." There is no way for me to know reliably how much people were holding back on my account. Racism has become so clearly socially unacceptable that even in this relatively safe, private environment, it may be impossible for people to say what they're really thinking. Or maybe it just does not matter all that much to them.

Predictably, the dealers were somewhat hostile toward the "black resistance culture," as sociologists sometimes call it, associated with rap, hip-hop, edgy fashion, and a sneering gangster attitude. Small wonder that white flea market dealers find this off-putting, especially those who associate unemployed blacks with welfare fraud. I suspect the rappers, hip-hoppers and gangsters would be disappointed if the dealers were not put off. But even here the dealers are mostly willing to treat individual cases individually. One dealer put it most bluntly: "I don't like niggers, but I would go into battle alongside any of the Africans selling beads in this market." (It's worth noting that virtually all of the bead-selling Africans are Muslim.)

The dealers face limited social consequences for being politically incorrect, but even they recognize that overt racism carries a significant social stigma. This is much less true about attitudes toward homosexuality. Gay marriage was the only issue on my list where a significant number of respondents were willing to say "no" to individual choice, to say gay people should not marry. But even on this most contentious of issues, a slim majority still said people should have a right to decide for themselves.

Cochise understood the economic and social realities all too well. Having married his former landlord, many years his senior, so she could get his health benefits, he understood why it mattered. "Why should a company, or the government, tell people who they can pick as their partner? If they've got a contract, as a couple, saying they'll share their worldly possessions, what difference does it make to anyone else what the two of them do in private? Do they go around checking whether husbands and wives have sex and how they do it? Then what do they care who I'm married to?"

As with black resistance culture, the dealers are wary of gay culture. Of course, they experience relatively little of it in southern Indiana. But they saw the heyday of *Will and Grace* and *Queer Eye for the Straight Guy* come and go, and they viewed both as an elite culture's attempt to force them to call homosexuality normal. "I don't care what they do, I swear I don't, but they don't have to rub my nose in it." In this case, they are the white working resistance culture, if such a thing can be imagined, pushing back against what they see as academic, intellectual, elite interests trying to sell them a bill of goods. As in every case, they feel put upon by blacks, Hispanics, gays, business moguls, and bureaucrats who are gradually chipping away at their "normal" way of life.

Among the middle classes, indeed even among some of the elite, the traditionalist and free market opinion-makers on one side slug it out with the toleration and interventionist opinion makers on the other. Fox battles MSNBC. Celebrities champion very different views of the world. But for the flea market dealers, the differences are often not so important. Celebrities touting politics have one thing in common: they are people with money who want to tell others what to do.

The realization that it doesn't matter all that much brings us back around to the underlying cause of the dealers' political disengagement: they are deeply cynical about the relationship between politics and money. *They are not on anybody's side because nobody is on their side.* They are irretrievably convinced that no one cares about their opinions or about how political and economic decisions affect them. And they are so clearly, obviously right about these things that those of us who imagine our views do matter should take a long look in the mirror and ask ourselves who is being fooled.

I ask myself the same question from time to time. I've had plenty of reason to think people pay some attention to some of my opinions. I write books, articles, and op-eds; at least a few people read these. My students have to pay attention to my lectures because I write the tests. My wife was, for a long time, a highly paid executive in a relatively small town, so local businesses and charities paid attention to us. And yet when I spend time with my dad and my flea market friends, I'm reminded how far they feel from power, how distant they are from the centers of control, and I wonder where I fall on the continuum running between very powerful and totally powerless.

The distinction was brought home to me once when we were sitting around the campfire at Friendship. We were talking about my wife's work and I mentioned how happy I was that sales were way up that year. A good friend asked, "What difference does that make to you? It's not like they're going to give her any of that money." It hit me like a truck that my friend had no idea how it worked, no clear concept that 50 to 70 percent of my wife's total annual compensation came from bonuses and stock options and was based entirely on her company's performance. She had a deep stake in the system that line workers cannot comprehend. Viewed from another perspective, she was the "they" in "they are always looking out for number one," no matter how nice I think she is and no matter how much she cared about the company's other employees.

In many ways, my wife and I moved toward membership in the elite, and yet I maintained a constant skepticism—bordering occasionally on cynicism—about both government and business. Despite my libertarian tendency to favor less government, I realize that government provides many things—defense, policing, roads, safety regulation of various kinds—that are more sensibly paid for by all citizens as a group than by individuals contracting with competing, private vendors. And I'm not tone deaf; I realize government sometimes redistributes income in ways that smooth over problems caused by inequality, especially the inequality bred by the social re-ordering caused by globalization. I received state and federal subsidies for my college education and I'm grateful for it. I know Social Security has nearly eliminated the worst poverty among senior citizens.

But at bottom, I do not think of government as an extension of myself and my neighbors. I do not view state or local governments as organizations that represent millions of us as one community. The military may represent our national interests, but in most other endeavors I think of my relationship to my neighbors as contractual—we have a deal about how we will treat one another and who will pay for what. That deal is not an empty shell based only on procedure. We do share values as fellow citizens, but these are mostly values that underscore the ability to choose for ourselves: limited, representative democracy; the rule of law; toleration; equal treatment under the law.

It's not that I cling to some atomistic vision of the isolated individual going it alone; I belong to many communities and am well aware of the ways in which they shape and sustain me and of my responsibilities within them. But I am leery of broad communitarian visions in which government, especially the federal government, provides the kind of planning, coordination, and regulation in which all of us are considered extended family members contributing to a common good. With only a few exceptions—again, national defense comes to mind— I'm not convinced we have a common good beyond our shared interest in freedom of choice, civil order, and equal treatment. At the very least, I'm not willing to let others define that common good for me. I'm not an organization man in government or in business.

Now imagine my flea market friends like Cochise. They honestly realize how limited their choices are. And for them it's not just the President or corporate big shots pulling the strings, but insurance adjustors, foremen from their previous jobs, bank tellers, cops, and preachers.

The dealers know their political opinions will never get heard over multi-million dollar ad campaigns. They know their job skills are easily replaced so employers view them as interchangeable resources. They know banks, insurance companies, law enforcement, retailers, zoning boards, and a host of other organizations set rules they cannot hope to change. And in all these things, they are correct, sanctimonious platitudes notwithstanding. They have no hope for causing social change; they resist by disengaging.

Ever wonder why working class and poor white people support conservative ideas—limited government and lower taxes—when a greater distribution of wealth would seem to be in their best interest? Why did so many of them resist health care reform when it would seem to benefit them considerably? Old-school Marxists would say it's because they do not understand their true interests and are kept from solidarity with others in their position. Cultural analysts might say nationalism or literal religious beliefs cause them to align on factors other than pure political or economic advantage. Free market defenders might argue that the poor hope to be rich some day and see free access and free trade as their best hope.

There may be some truth in all of those explanations, but let me offer a corrective that comes not from a distant, theoretical perspective, but out of the flea market dealers' daily experiences: *they want to be left alone.* Taxes are a form of control. Even when they aren't paying much tax, if any, they don't really imagine that the redistribution of wealth is coming toward them. Government programs are a form of control. To participate, one must get back in the line where others tell you what to do. If you trusted government and business, you might support policies designed to shift the system in your favor. But if you don't trust it at all, you are only looking for ways to limit its impact on your daily life.

I don't believe the flea market dealers are conservative. They are populists with no place to go and no hope of success. When a populist politician like Ross Perot or Jesse Ventura comes along whom they think might actually challenge the system, they'll engage. I cannot prove this now, but I suspect many of them voted for Obama when the economic chips were down. They weren't the only ones.

But short of real populism—and most of their options are far short of it—they'll disengage and take their chances with limited government. If the system is unlikely to work for you, the best you can hope for is to get as far from it as possible.

Not the Moral Majority

The dealers put the lie to the stereotypes about religion and politics. They are literalists about the Bible, but they are not part of the "evangelical" or "Christian conservative" movement in America, and not part of a Tea Party that combines evangelical fervor with libertarianism and state's rights. Just over 50 percent of my respondents favor a woman's right to choose an abortion. This may seem surprisingly high, but it really should not be. American attitudes toward abortion are connected to lifestyle, part of a whole way of life. That way of life is supported by institutions like churches, schools, magazines, and television programs. The flea market dealers are not part of that on either side.

For instance, those who take the side of individualism, and are generally more pro-choice, are likely to see a woman's role in the world tied to her chances to advance through business, education, and a co-equal role in the family. Pro-lifers, by contrast, are more likely to hold traditional views of women's roles and of family life, views supported by many churches, especially Catholicism and the conservative-evangelical wing of Protestantism. My respondents are not deeply rooted in any of those middle-class religious and institutional commitments; they are not morally or culturally defending bets that have already been placed. They are very simply weighing what seems like a moral tragedy against what seems like an individual's right to decide. Deep inside, all of us know that in that simple equation, stripped of all other social commitments, the scale is precariously balanced and our own dispositions often rest gingerly on one side or the other.

On other social issues, they have more lopsided opinions, but these can be seen in the same light. These folks oppose gun control about 4 to 1 or, if you prefer, they favor an unfettered right to keep and bear arms. As I interviewed in flea markets where guns are sold, this could hardly be otherwise. Dealers in urban flea markets are in fact more likely to suggest the need for some firearm restrictions. But it is important to note a greater uniformity here because in this case, unlike abortion, a conservative or traditional moral worldview does *not* butt up against the ideal of individual autonomy. With abortion, you can't have it both ways; you have to choose moral traditionalism or individual freedom. With gun control, you can have both on the same side.

In the outside world, "liberals" who favor stricter gun rules often operate from concerns about public health and safety and so are likely to view the body politic as a cooperating community. My respondents don't see it like that; for them, government is something acting *on* them, not something they act *within*. Public welfare is unlikely to trump their individual freedoms on guns, drugs, smoking, or almost any other issue.

Political Implications

It is a *typological* mistake for sociologists and theologians to lump all Bible-believers together under the rubric of "fundamentalism." Fortunately, the social costs of academic and intellectual errors are usually minor because few pay attention. But it is a *political* mistake of biblical proportions to write off all scriptural literalists as red-state, moral-values Republicans. Biblical literalists are not a monolithic group if they are indeed a group at all. A lot of literalists fall into the disconnected group represented by the dealers. Just as they are not Tea Partiers on the relationship between market and government, they are not Moral Majoritarians when it comes to religion and government.

Everyone knows a powerful bloc of committed Christians who are morally and biblically conservative has coalesced around pro-family, pro-life, pro-American, and anti-gay values. Like all political blocs, the contemporary Christian right has created an "us versus them," with "them" represented by social liberals, academics, gays, activist judges, and government bureaucrats. But the common man biblical literalists I talked to in the flea markets are *not* part of that bloc, at least not always. Admittedly, they are likely to share very conservative attitudes toward gays and lesbians who have not yet made inroads with the flea market, gun show, or NASCAR crowds, despite the past success of *Will and Grace* or *Queer Eye*. But on other issues, especially economics, they are more populist than the red-state stereotype of conservative evangelicals implies.

Recently there have been serious suggestions that voting can be predicted by knowing how someone feels about God, Guns, and Gays. If that simple equation holds true, then my respondents should be voting Republican. *But I simply have not seen that broad commitment to Republicans as a party or conservatism as an ideology across the board.* When Cochise thinks of "us and them," "them" is represented not by liberals and academics, but by everyone who bends the system to their benefit. He may have been convinced to distrust John Kerry as an east coast liberal and a Vietnam critic despite his Purple Hearts, but that does not mean he trusted George W. Bush as a God-fearing Christian. Who could be more a part of "the system" than a man who attended Yale and Harvard and whose own father is perhaps the best-connected man in America? The flea market crowd may not always know the difference between Iraq and Iran, as country singer Alan Jackson put it, but they know both George W. Bush and John Kerry were members of Skull and Bones at Yale, and none of them are surprised.

The ideal of freedom embodied in their rugged individualism is strong because it is a protective response allowing them to feel some sense of control in a situation where they have very little. The ideal provides them a narrative which makes order out of relative disorder. But this is a defense mechanism, not a deeply-held political conviction. A leader able to frame himself as an outsider capable of flattening the power of oligarchs and insiders could yet appeal to the populist instincts that lie just beneath the individualistic surface. Ross Perot tapped a nerve not so different from the one Huey Long tapped decades before. *The flea market literalists are not prone to political mobilization, but if it ever happens, it will be because a populist has pricked their fears, not because a religious conservative has stoked their zeal. Is there such a person, a populist who appeals to the dealers, the Tea Partiers, and to the young people who camped out on Wall Street?* Hard to imagine, but in the meantime, it is shortsighted to dismiss this multi-million-member chunk of Bible-believers as part of the "values voters" market segment.

Political opinions, religious opinions, and patterns of both voting and church attendance are not just outcomes of our *beliefs*, they are tokens of our *identity maintenance*. Most of the time, we think and do things not because we've spent a lot of time considering their philosophical consistency, but because that's the kind of people we want to be and want others to think we are. Not everyone who says the Bible is the "actual word of God and is to be taken literally" is certain they are right and they are even less interested in imposing this view on others through a systematic moral theology. The only thing many of them are certain of is that the rules—about politics, about religion, and about money—get made by someone else.

Biblical literalism is a train carrying a full load of cultural assumptions about right and wrong or good and evil. Sometimes the tracks lead to the politics of the Christian Coalition, but other times they lead to a church-going piety that says religion and politics should not mix. Still other times the tracks lead to an individualistic distrust of both church and politics. It is not enough to know that some people believe the Bible should be read literally or even that those same people share some core moral ideas about hot-button topics such as homosexuality. To understand how this set of beliefs translates into civic engagement or withdrawal, we must also know which ideas and social circumstances act as the switchmen.

Neither Republicans nor Democrats should assume that the common man's political allegiance is locked up. Biblical conservatism was a political watchword of the late 90s and early 2000s, but it is just one national, political fault line that must not be taken out of context. Some literalists do join Focus on the Family, but many others are populists or individualists searching vainly for candidates who speak to, and for, them.

The two take-away messages on flea market religion and politics should be clear:

First, don't assume that a person is a politically conservative evangelical just because he or she is a biblical literalist. It is just not that simple. There is a politically conservative, evangelical, subculture with its own books, magazines, television shows, and movies. But many people who believe the Bible literally are not part of that subculture.

Second, always remember that most people's tool boxes contain a hodgepodge of tools, not a matching set. The flea market dealers mix libertarian politics, populist economics, and literalist religion to create a worldview where folktales, biblical stories, supernatural mysteries, and fragments of common-sense wisdom (whether true or false) blend easily despite the occasional logical inconsistency.

Every tool in the toolkit is a bona fide piece of Americana. If it doesn't add up to a matched set, if it refuses to fit into our Red or Blue boxes, it could be because the ideas don't fit together. But maybe this isn't so much a problem with the toolkit—it works day to day—but a problem with the rational way we try to think about it. The hodgepodge, the lack of philosophical consistency, is probably more a problem for the observer than for the person being observed.

6

Cochise, Dad, and Me

A s I mentioned at the outset, I'm embarrassed by how far I got into this research before I realized how much of the task of writing this book would be about figuring out who I was. And it gets worse. I had not consciously considered the fact that my dad is a Biblical literalist, after a fashion, who doesn't trust the government and doesn't go to church. He made it further into the middle class than a lot of the dealers will, but when he was laid off from the power company for a while, he was a flea market dealer too.

There is no way for me to confront the flea market dealer's attitudes—Cochise's attitude—toward God, government, and freedom without confronting my own. I collect American "outsider" art, but I can keep the artists at arm's length, buying their art and reveling in its unselfconscious purity, remaining all the while on the other side of the looking glass. But I can't separate myself from Cochise so easily. Why do I share his distrust of government? How did I lose the built-in, culturally-conditioned belief in God he has? Can freedom mean the same thing to me it means to him? For him, freedom really is "just another word for nothing left to lose," but I've got plenty to lose. Can our sense of detachment be rooted in the same beliefs and fears or are there only surface similarities with different root causes?

Distrust of Government

My fear of government grows out of my distrust of "community" as a concept. Don't misunderstand me, I'm no misanthrope or radical revolutionary. You'll never read about me being shot by federal agents in a cabin like the one on Ruby Ridge. I have a very tight extended family and if one of my family members called me tonight I'd be there tomorrow with work boots on and checkbook in hand. I have maintained the same tight circle of friends since I left college twenty-eight years ago.

But I fear the ideological *concept* of community and do not think of the government as embodying community. I fear the concept of community being used to enforce beliefs and norms and mores, no matter whether this enforcement comes from social liberals or social conservatives. I acknowledge that there are things it makes sense for us all to do together as citizens: pay for the army, pay for roads, pay to guarantee educational access, and maybe even pay to guarantee health care. I'm hardly an ideologue on this and I get frustrated by those who are because nothing in our complex society could be so black and white. But I see our shared, common enterprises in government as a contract we all implicitly and explicitly sign on to, not as a communal obligation like the ones I have to my friends and family and neighbors. Modern society is just too big, too complex, too diverse to presume that we hold very many cultural norms, assumptions, and values in common. It may take a village to raise a child, but we don't live in villages any longer and our country of 300 million, much less our globe of 7 billion, bears no relationship to the village concept. We are interdependent, to be sure, but not in ways that could sensibly be called "relational."

We need some shared values and assumptions, of course, and we have them. In fact, we wrote them down. Life, liberty, pursuit of happiness. Freedom of speech, religion, and assembly. The right to bear arms. That sort of thing. Much past there, I'm inclined to resist.

Too often, Americans talk about government as if the problem was that we just can't get the right people in office. Their idea is that government is good in principle, but the people who win elections aren't smart enough or virtuous enough—you know, they'll get corrupted if they weren't corrupt already. And so on.

But that's not how I experience it. I think corruption is part of the package. "Power corrupts" is a useful reminder, no matter how clichéd.

Here's another, more recent, reminder: "when buying and selling are controlled by legislation, the first thing to be bought and sold are the legislators."

People ask me, "Do you trust business more than government?" I wouldn't put it like that, because I know how ruthless business can be. I would say instead that I trust the power, even the tyranny, of money more than I trust the power and tyranny of government because money is in principle available to everyone and will, over time, move from lower uses to higher ones despite corruption and frequent misuse. I don't believe either of those things is true about government. Worse, government has the coercive power of armies, police, and prisons. When business people act, even if they act badly, they are very clear about their profit motives. But in government people can do wrong under the pretense of altruistic motives, such as the "greater good of the community." A lot of my university friends are confident that the community, acting through democratic participation and republican representation, can manage this better than the marketplace. I tend to doubt it.

So I have to ask myself: Is this what Cochise thinks too, when he repeats the bumper-sticker slogan "I love my country but fear my government"? I don't think so. He's afraid the rich and powerful are going to squeeze him using government, business, and religion, but he'd be happy enough to have any of those three institutions use their power to help the little guy. He just doesn't expect it, so he chooses "being left alone" instead. His reaction is defensive. A wealth of behavioral studies suggest it is human nature to focus more on potential loss than potential gain (which is why stock market investors are more likely to sell in a panic but to buy over time), so there's little surprise that Cochise digs in when faced with uncertainty.

This is why poor people seldom band together behind very liberal candidates and would-be populists like Ross Perot or even John Edwards: they are skeptical of rich, powerful people truly championing their side. (John Edwards, at least, later gave them reason to think they were right to be skeptical.) Some might occasionally drift toward a genuine wild-card candidate like the widely-known professional wrestler Jesse Ventura in Minnesota, but that level of organized populist sentiment is rare.

So Cochise is afraid of the elite and I am afraid of the majority and the lure of high ideals. We both want to carve out a space for ourselves where we are buffered, at least a little, against plans made for us by others who presume to know what our values and ideals should be.

Honesty compels me to admit that Cochise's chances for carving out that space and staying independent are better than mine, though I wouldn't trade him places. I have more money and so have somewhat greater control over certain choices like where I live, what kind of car I drive, or where I go on vacation. But the fact I have some money means, by definition, that I am more engaged with the broader economic and political systems. The economy cannot be separated from political decisions, as the credit crisis of late 2008 taught us. American political and economic decisions cannot be separated from those in Europe, China, or India. The depth and complexity of these interrelationships make the long-term prospects for libertarianism and every other kind of individualism poor. We will still have some individual choices, but within ever more proscribed spheres of our lives. Seen in that context, those who limit their contact with external institutions as much as possible are the most likely to maintain some degree of independence from political power or authority.

I say "some degree" very intentionally, because it would be dangerous indeed to romanticize this arrangement. "Dropping out" may maximize independence from some kinds of governmental regulation, but it does so at the expense of most of life's other opportunities. Higher education is an avenue that leads to buy-in to the system. Economic upward mobility is a way to buy in to the system. Membership in an established religious organization is a way to buy in to the system. All of the values and organizations of middle class stability provide greater life chances, but also tighter ties to the interconnected web of social interaction on which they rest. You can't really just buy part of the package; it comes as a set.

Dropping out may loosen many of those ties, but most life chances disappear as well. And "the system," to stick with that vague term for economic, political, and cultural interdependence, continues to set the context in which even the hyper-individualist must operate.

Put another way, even the most disconnected individualist must buy and sell in a marketplace where consumers' desires and the price they will pay are embedded in the broader social web. Laws and regulations are set by a government embedded in that same web. Rare indeed is the chance to live outside those laws, or the person who would truly want to. Values are taught by an educational system and reinforced by media embedded in that same web.

So the outsider does not get to change the rules in any sense, only to try to soften or mitigate their effects on her or his own, individual life. Those who live within the system seek some softening or mitigation through a network of mediating institutions like churches and synagogues, families, and fraternal groups. The individualist seeks a buffer by trying to achieve separation on his or her own, with no chance for more than partial success.

My dad lives in a mobile home, a trailer, deep in the Hoosier National Forest in southern Indiana. He bought that trailer in 1999 as a place to escape on January 1, 2000—or Y2K. He does not live entirely outside the system—he still gets veteran's medical care and still has a little money in the stock market—but he is constantly distrustful.

He votes for culturally conservative political candidates. He would call himself independent, but he always votes Republican. In his mind, government taxes everyone much too much and spends the money on wasteful programs. If he had to name the three things he thought it most important for government to accomplish, I believe he would say (1) protecting his right to keep and bear arms, (2) keeping a strong military to defend America, and (3) reducing taxation by reducing government spending, probably in that exact order. He doesn't care much about the sexuality issues of abortion or gay marriage, but he doesn't really mind if candidates are morally conservative so long as they are right on the issues he cares about.

He is not wrong, then, to vote for Republican candidates for federal offices. But the political topsoil beneath him is crumbling into sand with each passing year. In a country, indeed a world, that is rapidly urbanizing, the right to own firearms will continue to be modified and eventually restricted, despite a recent court case that found in favor of Second Amendment individual freedoms against Washington D.C.'s restrictive laws. For rural folks, or those with rural roots, guns mean meat on the table, personal security, and a link to a frontier past. But rural folks are a dwindling minority, and an America where European descendants, white people, are the minority—now probably less than four decades away—will not care so much about the frontier past. In urban areas, at close quarters, guns may offer protection, but they also represent danger, fear, and violence. Restrictions will proliferate and grow over the coming decades.

The American military will not be fading any time soon, but the future looks more like continual engagement and less like the past few decades of military intervention built on the idea of American exceptionalism. Standing armies might be the last vestiges of parochialism in a globalizing world, but even armies cannot remain unaffected forever. We have seen only the earliest stages of global coordination of military efforts through the United Nations. Both economic and military activities of many nations are destined to be managed under a much larger, international umbrella.

For readers who are already noting the code words of "American exceptionalism," "gun restrictions," "United Nations," and "global coordination" or "global economy," let me be blunt: this is not an underhanded jab at either the demographic change toward a European minority in the U.S. or at the mission of the United Nations. These are simply statements of what I see as the realities of globalization. I'm not offering any judgment at all about whether these processes are morally or practically good or bad for most human beings in the long run; I'm saying I think they are inevitable and they will work against traditional myths of liberalism or individualism, including the myth of American frontier self-reliance and the myth of full economic liberty in an Adam Smith-style capitalism. Globalization is happening; by definition, it means the death of individualism and, on a smaller scale, the end of the redneck, John Wayne, bootstrap myth as a subset of individualism. Ideologies change to meet the economic and demographic facts on the ground.

As for taxes, the other myth of America as a free-market economy has likely already outlived its usefulness. Again, please don't misunderstand: I think America will remain *more* market-oriented than most other countries, and I certainly hope it does. I tend to believe economic growth and expansion is best for everyone, even when it leads to greater inequality. But the idea that the world is divided into countries with totally free, laissez-faire markets on the one hand, or totally centralized, command economies on the other, is no longer even a useful fiction.

For instance, in America something like 25 percent of our GDP goes through the government. That percentage is closer to 50 percent in countries like Sweden, somewhat closer to 45 percent in France or Germany and more like 35 percent in Britain. But the most socialist society in Europe—even the largest Communist country of China—still participates in the market economy, even though the share taken from market processes and redistributed by government is higher. And in free-market democracies, such as the U.S., the government still takes and redistributes, although the share is lower. But it's not all-or-nothing and has not been for decades: it is more-or-less. The labels help nothing.

In the coming decades, America will inevitably move in the direction of greater government regulation and a greater share of GDP passing through governments' hands, current Republican attempts to halt that advance notwithstanding. The Congressional Budget Office estimated in 2002 that by 2075 government's share of GDP will be closer to 40 percent. We will continue to debate this process and to adjust policy on a case-by-case basis, but the notion that we are eighteenth- or even nineteenth-century pure capitalists barely merits continued discussion.

I don't mean to turn this into an economic analysis, but rather to make the point that the self-sufficient, laissez-faire individual is already an artifact. Social life is moving in the direction of greater mechanical connectedness and interdependence. As this change occurs and government grows, people like Cochise, the dealers, Dad, and me will feel more and more out to sea. The Tea Partiers represent a middle-class, largely evangelical, resistance to this shift, but they are trying to build a wall of sand to hold back the ocean.

Tens of millions of Americans already feel alienated from the governmental and economic structures within which they live daily. Indeed, many polls suggest the majority of Americans feel this way, so the flea market dealers are just a particularly striking example of an endemic problem. Globalization and greater government coordination will make some of the disaffected feel less alienated, but it will make others—rednecks among them—feel more alienated. Some fraction of the alienated will rebel through political or economic activism; most will muddle through discontentedly. A relatively small group will try to distance themselves entirely, as the dealers do. I am sympathetic to their sense of alienation and to their choices, but hardly optimistic about their prospects.

Belief and Distrust

The question of God is less prosaic, but worth the effort to consider. Cochise, like almost all the dealers, expresses the opinion that God is real and interprets events in his life as being caused by God. I don't. Most of the dealers believe God intervenes in the world on a regular basis. I don't. Most of the dealers are comfortable with a magical, or at least fateful, view of wealth or health. I'm not. The difference is clear. But what accounts for it?

To answer that question, it is important to keep in mind that it is not only possible, but normal, to maintain traditional, pre-scientific, pre-rational, pre-cynical worldviews in some spheres of life but not in others. Put another way, much of our world may operate on a theoretical, rational, basis, but this does not mean the old mythological bases have disappeared. In the institutionalized spheres of their lives—business, education, government, church—the dealers have taken a beating. They have been worn down by bureaucracy and capitalism and cronyism and elitism and by either their lack of desire to work within the system or their lack of ability to do so successfully. More often than not, they are blank-faced realists.

The traditional moorings that might once have held Cochise and his friends to the place of their birth and their extended families have been wrenched loose. This has happened to millions and millions of Americans, especially as they move from rural areas towards cities and suburbs, but most people reconnect themselves through schools, churches, jobs, civic groups, neighborhoods and other institutions.

Living on the edges of those institutions—and in some cases outside them altogether—Cochise has no place to drop anchor. To the extent the institutions governing his life are organized in an impersonal, rational, efficient fashion and advancement is by merit, he is out of luck. To the extent these institutions are based on connections, birthright, and cronyism, he is also out of luck.

But not so with God. God represents the possibility that there is compassion and fairness and justice in the world even though human beings may screw it up. And this isn't just the Big Rock Candy Mountain where we'll all go to heaven by and by when we die. I am leery of attempts to define religion as other-worldly compensation. Most of the dealers have a day to day apprehension that God watches out for the little guy. How else could they get out of bed every morning?

But that's not there for me. For me, the same forces of impersonal rationality that leave me at a detached distance from government—the contract metaphor rather than the family or village metaphor—leave me equally detached from God. I cannot be a true believer, no matter how much I want to feel it in my gut. And I do want to feel it. I have spent a lifetime pursuing religion because I remember what it felt like when it was deeply real to me and I am fascinated by, even envious of, others who still feel it.

I'm hardly a nihilist or even a hard-baked cynic. I believe "enough" on some matters. I believe in America as a project. I'm even patriotic, at least in the sense I think my country gets it right more than it gets it wrong. I feel an obligation to hold up my end of the social contract and to meet my citizen obligations, even if I think of them as part of an implied contract rather than some communal requirement. I want to thank and reward those who sacrifice on my behalf, including those who serve in the military, even if it means money taken from my pocket. I don't want to be a free rider.

But this sense of citizenship is a detached, rational sense of obligation, not the emotional, core-of-my-being kind of thing I feel toward my wife and kids. With them it's a vow constituting who I am; with patriotism, it's just a frame of reference and I'm always self-conscious that it could be otherwise. With religion, for me, it's not even a frame of reference.

The dealers believe in many variations of folk religion, most including plenty of conservative Christian belief. My dad falls into the same category. They all believe God created the world, in the absence of a more compelling story. (And trust me here: the current telling of the story of natural selection and adaptation is not compelling at the popular level, which is why fewer than 20 percent of Americans believe in evolution without divine influence.) They believe God wants to help them or sends guardian angels to watch over them or is interested in the minute details of their daily lives. They believe Jesus was raised from the dead because, well, because that's what "normal" people believe. When and where they grew up, everyone believed this. Amazingly, in a world where atoms can be split and humans walked on the moon more than forty years ago, disbelief on core "facts" like these can still make you an outsider in many circles.

Do the dealers *really* believe? Does Cochise? Does my dad? Not to become overly academic, but it genuinely depends on what you mean by "believe." In one sense, they believe more than most churchgoers I come into contact with on a regular basis. I know many intelligent, well-read people who remain faithful in the midst of considerable doubt. The dealers are not having the same psychic struggle. They believe in the simple sense of acceptance or intellectual assent because competing worldviews are not constantly bombarding them, at least not in any way they consciously realize. So if belief means "accepting that something is true," they believe.

But in another way, they believe less than my faithful friends. My churchgoing friends are believers in the sense they have made a choice or have adopted a lifestyle—whether they consciously made an adult decision or took on the ascribed status of their upbringing. They "believe" in the sense that their actions match up to their ideas. I'm not saying they are always consistent—who is?—but they work within the framework of faith. So if belief means "living a life of faith," then maybe not so much for the dealers.

Cochise and his friends are quick to call many churchgoers, and especially pastors, "hypocrites" and to accuse them of being concerned only about money or appearances. And no doubt sometimes this criticism is correct. The flesh is weak. But from another point of view, the dealers are hypocrites too. They say they believe in God and believe the Bible is God's infallible word, but they do not study the Bible—don't even read it—and don't belong to communities of believers trying to support one another. They do not make any special effort to exhibit Christ-like characters, although many would say they do strive to live up to the baseline values of love, charity, and justice.

I don't call anyone a hypocrite, at least not on this account. There are not many Gandhis or Mother Teresas in the world. People do the best they can. The overwhelming majority of adherents of all faiths all over the world venerate ideals that provide a framework to make sense of their lives day to day. Cochise is no different, but his beliefs are not reinforced through study or discipline, so it is that much harder for him to support a worldview not really grounded in other kinds of commitments either.

My beliefs are tremendously different from theirs, exposing the chasm that lies between who I once was and who I am now, or between myself and my dad or Cochise. I do not believe in God as a matter of unselfconscious assent. I have made a conscious, rational decision not to live "in faith," despite the fact my life would be simpler in many ways if I did. I was destined for ordained ministry. My family expected faith from me. I could have lived my life comfortably ensconced in a tight framework of related ideas, opinions, and actions. I could, at the very least, have lived in the hope of the resurrection.

I have no interest in portraying myself as some heroic figure who threw off the shackles; that is not what happened. I just learned to frame the question about God as an argument and then, over time, came to believe that the weight of evidence was on the side of non-believers despite the fact they were a small minority in my subculture, the broader American culture, and the entire world. I respect people of faith, but am more persuaded if their faith is based on the hope of belief—on trust—not on full, conscious assent. But there needs to be something there; I have little interest in people who participate in religious myth and ritual only, consciously, for its functional qualities.

For myself, I will not make Pascal's famous wager that it is better to live as if there were a God. I cannot live my life "as if" based on hope or trust. I appreciate what a wonder existence is—that there is something rather than nothing in the world—but this alone does not lead to faith or discipline or morality in any sensible way I can imagine. I just try to maintain a sense of curious awe.

Having already stated my case that interdependence and globalization will mean the end of individualism or even the myth of individualism—whether the dealers' or my own—I feel some obligation to say whether I think the religious worldview or the rational, empirical worldview will win out in the end. I wish I knew.

Half a century or more ago, theorists in my field predicted human society would gradually move toward more reliance on reason, empiricism, and science, and away from faith, spirituality, or magic. Religionists and religion scholars are both quick to point out gleefully that people are at least as personally religious now as they ever were. And these gloaters are right.

But I don't think this means the theories—usually called secularization theories—were entirely wrong. Yes, the large majority of people did leave a place in their lives for religion or spiritualism or mysticism or whatever, but they live most of their lives in spheres that have become thoroughly secular and increasingly based on reason, science, and, perhaps most of all, economic and political efficiency governed by bureaucracies.

Very little in American public life is based on magic or a sense of the supernatural, despite the fact the majority does "believe" in the supernatural. Our Constitution quite intentionally limits government's ability to base its decisions or actions on religion. And gradually, religion has moved out of public life—whether political, economic, educational, or leisure—and into the realm of private individuals, their families, and their chosen communities. In the bigger communities or organizations where people must interact with strangers—and most of us in an urbanized nation have the majority of our interactions with relative strangers—religion has been pushed aside.

Think about it. Religion has been almost entirely excised from the public schools. In battles between religion and other spheres of human experience, religion has lost. Religion can rarely be used as a legal legitimization for drug use, animal cruelty in rituals, or non-standard military uniforms. In most cases, religion gives way. It's okay to be religious, but that does not excuse anyone from following all the secular, rational, bureaucratic rules.

When I was a kid, liquor was not sold on Sundays anywhere. Now many states allow the unfettered sale of alcohol, and virtually all states allow it to be sold in restaurants. Just a few decades ago, stores were closed to observe the Sabbath. No longer. Sermons from pastors of important congregations were published in the newspaper. Not anymore. Towns held joint worship services to celebrate Easter or Christmas and had Sunday school parades. Now the holiday celebrations are rare and the parades are simply gone. In a pluralizing, secularizing culture these changes away from religion were inevitable, not least because of the legal protections for religious minorities. I am not complaining about these changes, I am simply describing them.

Religion moved out of the realm of our broader, impersonal social interactions but stayed vital at the smaller, more local level. More than a few Americans see this as bad—they wish religion would play a larger role in our public lives—but I think most Americans see this change as beneficial. Who really wants religionists—especially religionists who believe something different from what you believe—to be able to set moral standards for everyone? Who really thinks, for instance, that revolutions in Muslim countries aimed at re-instituting conservative Sharia law are a good thing? Almost no one I know. Most Americans think religion is working fine when it provides meaning—and therapy—for individuals, their families, and their chosen groups of fellow believers. They are leery of seeing it publicly promoted and genuinely hostile to the notion of it being forced down anyone's throat.

I see these developments as part of a long—very long—march in the direction of rationality and secularization. I wish I could be optimistic or enthusiastic about this—especially since it moves in the direction of the secular, rational position I have accepted for myself—but two very different counter-points give me pause.

First, belief in magic and spirituality has proven incredibly resilient, resisting the breathtaking advance of science. Americans have seen a man walk on the moon, yet the majority believes heaven is a real place. Evolution based on variation, adaptation, and natural selection has become the dominant metaphor in biology, yet millions of Americans believe God created Adam and Eve in a garden. The earth is known to be over 4 billion years old, yet more than 40 percent of Americans believe it was created in the past few thousand years in pretty much its present form.

But the persistence of magic and spirituality is not just about the irrational and ill-informed. Well-educated people believe they have guardian angels, crystals and pyramids have special powers, or God intervenes in their daily lives to heal sickness or prevent injury. Beyond even this, though, is the basic faith in God as creator and sustainer, a faith shared by the large majority of Americans. People live in a world where science explains more and more of what was once interpreted by religion, a world where political and economic bureaucracies govern more and more of their lives, yet their faith in a higher power somewhere above it all persists.

The second reason I resist the urge to cheer secularization is that rationalization and bureaucratization pose significant problems of their own. Max Weber pointed out better than anyone what life in the "iron cage" of rationality might look like. A world without magic or spirituality could be pretty bleak, which is probably why I buy artwork by true believers. Yes, therapy is available in secular forms, but is that what the future holds: ever more nuanced attempts to protect our fragile psyches from the impersonal forces of political and economic realities?

By this point, it has no doubt dawned on most readers that I am not the first person to experience the angst of modern, or, God help us, postmodern, existence. I'm not the first person to note the contemporary existential crisis. But I might be the first person to use flea market dealers and their detachment from civil society to approach alienation and to think about my own place in the world.

And thus we come to freedom. Cochise didn't want to have a boss, who is after all the symbol of involuntary, even irrational, control. Cochise is severely controlled by his circumstances—most notably his lack of resources—but that control seems less tyrannical because he still gets to make the little choices about when to open his booth, what clothes to wear, how to style his hair, and so on. He is allowed at least the trappings of individual control. To be honest, he gets to control the same personal lifestyle details the rest of us get to control in a consumerist society. But he cares less what the fashion is and so he is not always hurtling toward the next new thing.

Redneck culture reflects this. You may think the gun ownership attachment—and the knee-jerk reaction to any proposal of gun control—is some kind of Freudian projection. Not me. I think it is about a particular kind of freedom. A gun is a link to that frontier past, a tie to the Daniel Boone and Davy Crockett myths. But more than that, a gun, at bottom, means the ultimate ability to say "no" to coercion. It is the bottom line on what political scientists call "negative freedom" or "freedom from."

But a gun only spares you from direct, personal coercion. Most people are more afraid of direct, personal crime—assault or mugging—than they are of white collar crime, even though the white collar variety costs them much more in the long run. Same deal here. A gun is freedom, at least a little, from that kind of personal fear. But a gun won't keep global economics and politics from changing the entire context of our lives. So a gun is freedom, but the range of freedom is circumscribed by ever-shrinking boundaries imposed by huge, impersonal forces beyond any individual's control.

Still, like growing long hair and being able to tell the old boss to kiss your ass, guns are a measure of individual choice and individual liberty. It may not be much freedom, but it may be all there is left. In the end, that is why you will have to pry the guns from Cochise's, Dad's, or my cold, dead fingers.

So we all have at least this in common: we all see a world where institutional rules and expectations shape our lives more than we'd like. We are all detached from some of the social, cultural moorings that would make us feel more tied to and part of institutional life. We all feel alienated, in our own way. When you believe in and accept the shared, core values, you are part of a common enterprise, a member of the community, an actor in the great cosmic play, a puzzle-piece in God's plan. But when you are detached from that emotional and spiritual linkage, you are only a cog in the machine. That is why I envy true believers, even though I can never be one.

Like Cochise and the dealers, I may not be able to control the institutional forces, but I can try to limit their ability to control me. But here it is easiest to see the differences and difficulties between me and the dealers. They try to lighten the grip of institutions by refusing to participate to whatever degree they can. Yes, they are controlled by economic trends, but they don't punch the clock. Yes, they are controlled by social norms, but they don't have to sit in church on Sunday while a preacher tells them what's what. Yes, they are controlled by the political environment, but they don't have to give politicians the satisfaction of their consent. They were never going to be elites, or even mid-level managers, in the bureaucracy. They refuse to be organization men on the lowest rung.

But unlike them, I have money. Success for me has come—and probably must come—through institutional forms, even if I try to hold those institutions at arm's length (say, by avoiding supervisory jobs, voting libertarian, avoiding shopping malls and designer clothes, etc). But I've got to be honest: I get the benefits from a lot of those things by proxy, so I'm probably mostly just kidding myself. Still, I have done what I could to lessen their grip.

It would be tempting to conclude by saying what a wonderful thing freedom is, but I promised this would not be a romantic rendition of individualism. In an interdependent world, the struggle for individual freedom, existential freedom, can be pretty harsh. Take a hard look at Cochise. He does not work 9 to 5, does not have to wear ties, and does not have to kiss the butt of any boss, preacher, or politician. And what did life give him in return? A daily struggle to put food on the table and a pervasive sense of detachment and anomie.

My dad? He is retired now and lives life on his own terms. But he spends most of his days alone in his trailer talking to his beagle. He is not constrained by any social or religious organization. His life is defined by political and economic changes far beyond his control, but no more than anyone else's. The difference is, he assumes his voice cannot be heard, so he does not waste a lot of effort.

And me? In a lot of ways, my life *is* liberated. I've mostly worked when I wanted on what I wanted. Remember, I got a grant to study flea markets. Even when I have real jobs, I approach them as an independent contractor. My family situation mocks the traditional social roles that were handed to me; I stayed home with my kids while my wife chased the brass ring. I also do not have to kiss the butt of any boss, preacher, or politician—though I do have a wife.

So I lack many of the traditional social shackles too: I'm not an organization man, not even in religious organizations. But this involves a trade-off, because I also lack the sense of belonging and comfort and assurance that comes from being embedded in a system of beliefs and an integrated social worldview. If being free means being left alone, it also means being alone.

Not in the personal sense, of course. I love my friends and family and they love me. But in the larger sense, I'm detached from the confidence, the faith, that I am created, shaped and defined by my vocation, by my nation, or by God.

And that is where I have to acknowledge the most fundamental difference between Cochise and me: he is trying to protect his individualism and moral agency from a system that has boxed him out and pushed him aside. The system laid itself out at my feet and yet gradually, rationally, intellectually I detached myself from it. Cochise absorbed anomie and alienation, even if he does not consciously think about it. I have the uneasy sense I chose it. Unfortunately, once that genie is out of the bottle, it does not go back in. I know I am not a true believer in America or in God. I refuse to live my life "as if."

www.ingramcontent.com/pod-product-compliance
Lightning Source LLC
Chambersburg PA
CBHW020205090426
42734CB00008B/948